making **music**

Dedicated with love to Johanna
without whom neither
Kent Opera nor this book
would have existed

Norman Platt

Foreword by Nicholas Hytner

I am indebted for informed suggestions to
Claire Seymour and Lucinda Platt.
Norman Platt

First published in Great Britain in 2001 by
Pembles Publications,
Pembles Cross Farmhouse, Egerton,
Ashford, Kent TN27 9BN
Fax 01233 256704

Extract from *Metaphysics as a Guide to
Morals* by Iris Murdoch published by
Chatto & Windus. Used by permission of
The Random House Group Limited.

Title page illustration of the Fenice poster
used by kind permission of John Ward.

Jacket illustration courtesy of Jane Lewis.

Designed by Andrew Barron &
Collis Clements Associates.

Printed and bound in England by
Butler & Tanner Limited.

ISBN 0954128702

9 780954 128708

Contents

6 I was impelled to write this book by a sense of the need to praise, preserve and explain the art of music, which for various reasons is under great threat. I deal with music: its meaning, its relationship to words, its vulnerability to ignorance, its performance and its funding. And I use the experience of one professional lifetime as a framework. This is why opera (which does in fact contain every other form of music writ large) takes the dominant part in the discussion.

Foreword by Nicholas Hytner

During the twenty years of its existence under Norman Platt's direction, Kent Opera was like the city that is set on an hill. It could not be hid.

Its resources were focused on truthful, musical and completely alive performances. It ruthlessly refused to have anything to do with the meretricious or the frivolous, either in its choice of repertoire or in the way it dealt with the works it chose to produce. It made no compromises with its audiences, still less with the authorities whose mission it was to dilute or eliminate the excellent in the name of accessibility. But through its shining integrity, it made better opera more accessible to more parts of the country than anyone has managed since.

Those of us who were lucky enough to attract Norman's attention know that we will never again do work of such concentrated dedication to what is valuable and beautiful. It was simply impossible to imagine presenting to Norman cheap or fashionable solutions to the challenges he made to us.

His fascinating book explains why from his earliest encounters with music, at Bury Grammar School and at Bayreuth (a combination of influences of which few other musicians can boast), he has clung passionately to the belief that it provides an image of virtue. In the name of virtue he sought out the best in the musical and operatic worlds, did battle with the funding authorities, and even mortgaged his house. Never for him the cynical programming of a chic new production of *Tosca* to pull in the crowds.

Norman's accounts of the many pinnacles of Kent Opera's two decades are vital and unfailingly generous to the talented and dedicated crew he formed around him. They bring back for me the best experiences I had working in opera, and some of the best I have had watching it. I have never collaborated with a conductor as happily or as productively as I did with Roger Norrington or Ivan Fischer; indeed, it might be truer to say that only at Kent Opera have I encountered the idea that the relationship between conductor and director should genuinely be a collaboration, rather than a mutual staking out of territory, sometimes genial, sometimes not.

It is impossible not to share Norman's cold fury at the destruction of the company by precisely those who must have felt most undermined by its rigorous refusal to deal with what Norman calls 'the fading fad of relativism (ie. the view that everything is equally good, equally trivial, equally bad, equally valuable).' But it's precisely for this reason that I hope this book is widely read by those in the performing arts, and particularly by those who come to watch and listen. Norman only cares for what is good. For too long now we have been giving our audiences the popular and the successful, but we're in danger of forgetting that subsidised art is subsidised so that it doesn't have to worry about anything except excellence.

This book, like Norman's life, is about how to achieve it.

Nicholas Hytner

King Priam Tippett (1985) with Janet Price as Athene, Howard Haskin as Paris, Anne Mason as Aphrodite and Sarah Walker as Hera

Music and Meaning

In the beginning was the Cry: the cry of confidence, of recognition, of hope, of joy, the cry of pain, the cry of fear, the cry of anger, the cry of despair.

Underneath was the cruel will to survive, unexplained.

Later came the Word: the naming of things and of actions, of creatures and ideas, and the undeniable utility and apparent sense of control such naming brought.

From the shaping and refinement of the primitive cry came music. From the endless re-ordering and organisation of the names came poetry.

Neither poetry nor music fill the belly nor do they seem to nurture power over the environment nor that ruthless will to survive. So why are they there?

Poetry achieves its aims by seeking to attain the instinctual ground from which music springs: by such methods as the musical elements in its own material, rhythm, metre, sometimes rhyme; by the overtones (a musical metaphor) which every word adds to itself minute by minute and perhaps most of all by the fresh and revelatory ordering of

From the slow movement of Schubert's string quintet in C major, opus D956 its utilitarian components. When Hamlet begs Horatio *Absent thee from felicity awhile* it means more, much more, than 'Please don't die yet' – and also has the weight of three and a half hours worth of other perceptions and revelations behind it; and when Perdita offers: *Daffodils That come before the swallow dares and take The winds of March with beauty* – she is saying not simply something different but also so much more than 'Have a nice flower'. The sense, shape, sound, rhythm and significance of her words are indissoluble and inseparable and cannot be paraphrased. They say something appropriate to that moment in the drama and simultaneously universalise that moment and lift it (and us) out of time.

Music, starting from the other end, seeks structure: a grammar, syntax and forms appropriate to itself. It conveys a message and/or meaning that cannot be conveyed otherwise.

Western music is an art of sound grounded in what is known as the tonal system. This is a system which evolved over several centuries and is based on a relationship between various pitches notably the octave (described by Blom as 'the most astonishing phenomenon in acoustics') and the fifth. There were also various human adjustments or nudges to the intervening gaps and these adjustments eventually produced what is known as Equal Temperament.

The meaning in music is not the same as verbal meaning: it comes from the cry and not from the word. The concept of the *language* of music is one that should be used very, very rarely and with great caution. Though there is from time to time an obvious overlap, there is never an identity between the Word and the Cry.

The two arts – music and poetry – are in fact on a cross-flow; and where they join a third art is created – song, cantata, oratorio, opera; the art of the 'sphere-born harmonious sisters, Voice and Verse'. No-one would be so foolish as to claim that music is, per se, a 'greater' art than poetry: indeed, as I have said, the miracle of great poetry is that it can employ utilitarian materials to attain the instinctual and non-utilitarian ground where music lives. The priority of music when combined with words is demonstrable by the fact that though you can have a great song with weak words (Schubert repeatedly proved it) you cannot have a great song with weak music. And although opera is a more complicated matter it is worth remarking that the gates of Heaven will not open to the most perceptive and committed reading of a libretto by the gifted da Ponte; add Mozart's music and those same gates immediately fly apart. And you remember Busenello? You don't? – a great librettist hanging on to immortality through the genius of Monteverdi.

So how does music itself work? Dipping a tentative toe into these deep and risky waters one can hazard the following statements. In music the primitive cry is refined, without distorting its truth, into a rhythmic shape of sensuous delight. A series of such shapes is joined both horizontally (melody) and vertically (harmony) and both at once (counterpoint) to form a larger shape. And all the separate shapes are related to one another, like close or distant members of a family.

13

Filling a period of time with these larger shapes in a satisfying manner is analogous to the filling of space in a satisfying manner by a painter. The important thing about music is that just as painting however abstract is related to things seen and felt, so music, however refined and subtle, is related to cries which emerge from meaningful experiences deep within the human psyche and which cannot be expressed so well in any other way. The fitting together of the various elements in music (melody, counterpoint, rhythm etc) demands great skill; and one of the satisfactions of listening to music is the pleasure occasioned by observing how well the craftsman solves his problems. But with great works the felicity of the solutions and the quality of the vision they present transport us to a new level of awareness – as did Perdita's daffodils. For good art truthfully encompasses and transcends all manner of human experience. It enables us to bear the unendurable, to learn and grow from the joyful and to make sense of the apparently senseless.

That is what it is there for.

Personal preface and credentials

A north-country industrial town in the early 1920s tended to make   **15**
the inhabitants walk with head down, not looking at their
surroundings; it did not discourage them from hearing and making
music.

My father always sang about the house; my mother, claiming to
have been mocked for her singing in early marriage, never gave voice
again. Though neither of my parents could play, they bought a piano
in anticipation of children who would learn. And play we did, both
my elder brother Edward and myself.

Both my parents had known poverty in childhood: my mother,
who loved learning, was sent to work in a Lancashire cotton mill from
the age of twelve; my father, who had wanted to be an accountant,
humped heavy suitcases round as a travelling salesman until he had
saved enough to found his own Tea Merchant business. Both were
determined that their two sons should have all that they had lacked.

My first sense of music as something 'other' was at the age of four
as I was getting up one morning: a sound which outdid the rival
noises coming from the slipper-works across the back and the jingling

The Magic Flute Mozart, Bury Grammar School (1931) with Norman Platt as Parmina of the horse-drawn milk-cart at the side caused me to stand transfixed and barefoot at the top of the stairs. It was the gramophone playing the overture to *The Mikado*: (the initial strangeness of the 'Japanese' modality followed by the jolly tonal music?). A strange choice for a profoundly important experience. However: 'Play that again' I called out in a firm, bossy voice, 'I like that'; and played again it was. (There was, I think, only one occasion on which my father refused me a musical request: but that came much later.) His favourite composer, played on the gramophone, or, later, heard on the wireless but above all sung by himself about the house in a smooth, expressive baritone was Handel. Indeed all the really great composers (how many? ten – a dozen?) all seem to have made their entry into my consciousness in organised succession when I was ready to receive and absorb them: and my father's Handel proved a sound foundation for all that was to follow – quite apart from that composer's individual greatness.

16

I have been unable to imagine life without music and I owe this necessary wonder, this continually renewed discovery, to many people, some still alive, most of them dead.

In 1927, at the age of six I started my piano studies with Annie Hunt, my brother's teacher. Highly regarded both as player and teacher, she lived in a small house with her sickly mother upstairs and two pianos in her small sittingroom downstairs. Above one of these pianos there hung a picture of Brahms playing something showy with crossed hands; and on that piano stood a picture of a young man who had been killed in the war. The war was a subject which was rarely, if ever, mentioned at that time.

There was, for obvious reasons, little or no development in my understanding of Handel in my first year or two at Miss Hunt's. Instead, after the preparatory 'learning' pieces – Walter Carroll etc – a great influx over the next few years of the simpler pieces of Mozart and Haydn; and so on to the never simple pieces of Beethoven and

Brahms, who was Miss Hunt's great idol. She was a very good teacher and her enthusiasm never flagged. Out of teaching hours there was also much duet and even eight-handed playing on the two pianos in which older and more experienced friends joined favoured pupils. There was never, as I remember, a feeling of boring effort involved, just lots of concentration, discovery and delight. And the four- and eight-handed versions of symphonies gave one an intimate awareness of their structure long before one heard them with full orchestra, either on the wireless or nine miles away at Manchester's Free Trade Hall with the Hallé.

Handel returned, together with many new musical riches, when I entered, almost simultaneously, Bury Grammar School and Bury Parish Church Choir in 1929. The choir was my first 'paid job' and thus I became a professional musician (with extra half crowns for weddings and shillings for funerals) at the age of nine. The posts of music-master at the school and choir-master at the church were held by the same person – Dr Walter Williams, a very remarkable musician and a very remarkable person. The Handel which he brought back to my attention was of course the Handel of the oratorios: Handel's operas, which were to become so important later in my life were virtually unknown in this country to everyone except perhaps the Kitchings and Edward Dent (Winton Dean hadn't even started on his great work). But in addition there was music from the sixteenth century to the twentieth, up to Martin Shaw and Vaughan Williams; this included many late nineteenth century works; the Psalms; and above all J S Bach, especially his *Matthew Passion* for which a section of the Hallé Orchestra was introduced into Bury Parish Church.

In his persona at the Grammar School, Dr Williams introduced other wonders, most notably a production, performed by the boys, of *The Magic Flute*, in which I, at the age of eleven, sang the part of Pamina. I could also sing the Queen of Night and much regretted that, as they both shared a scene, I could not sing both in the same performance. So I chose Pamina. I think one of Dr Williams' great

secrets of success was that he never suggested to young performers
that anything was difficult. He filled me, for one, with a love for that
impossible musical form, opera, that caused me so much delight and
pain at a later date. But that was not the end of Dr Williams by any
means. Later I decided to take music as one of my subjects for what
was then called the Higher School Certificate and for this I had the
luxury and privilege of studying with him as his only school pupil.
Although I rather resented some of his criticisms of my compositions
I enjoyed the lessons immensely, especially as I had by now decided
to become a composer.

The great upheaval occurred, not only for him but also for his
friends and students, when some time in his early sixties he discovered
Wagner. As a result I played again and again (from piano scores) every
note that Wagner wrote from the beginning of *The Flying Dutchman*
to the end of *Parsifal*, singing most of the parts.

18 For the next few years Wagner upset my musical equilibrium
quite badly, especially after Walter Williams invited me to accompany
him to Munich and Bayreuth to hear the real thing. He usually took
a companion with him on these pilgrimages and on this occasion it
was a 15 year old schoolboy. The year was 1936 and both Dr Williams
and I were about equal in our political unawareness. The first opera
I ever saw was Gluck's *Alceste*; but usually it was Wagner, sandwiched
between performances of Mozart and Richard Strauss. I recall these
performances (I think accurately) under such conductors as Böhm,
Strauss, and when we got to Bayreuth, Furtwängler, as being of an
orchestral splendour and subtlety such as I had never heard before
and with singing, production and acting of a very high quality.

The most shattering and dangerous musical experience of my
life was probably *Tristan and Isolde*, my first Wagner opera.

The ecstatic diary entry of my 15 year old self ends with a
view that was the same that I hoped for when I started to form
an opera company more than 30 years later: 'But the perfection of
the individual was swallowed up in the perfection of the whole:

singers, orchestra, design, everything joined together to achieve
a marvellous unity.'

It was at this point that I did not decide – I knew – that I would
one day have a son called Tristan.

When we got to Bayreuth for the end of the Festival
performances of Lohengrin and Parsifal, Dr Williams managed to
get us into 'Wahnfried', trading on his name (Winifred Wagner was
originally Winifred Williams). We were ushered through the room
where Parsifal was composed, past Wagner's piano and into the garden
where we met Wagner's daughter-in-law. I had by that time studied
enough Mozart and Beethoven to discourage my own ambitions as
a composer and had decided instead to be a conductor; I announced
this intention to a gravely attentive Winifred Wagner. This charming
and terrifying woman I later discovered had been until the previous
day hostess to Adolf Hitler.

I returned home, ecstatically, to be faced by a rather unexpected
and complete refusal of my parents to countenance the idea of my
becoming a professional musician. They pointed to the indisputable
truth (which my own experience has long supported) that the
performing arts are the most insecure financially of all professions.

It so happened that at this very moment my headmaster,
Mr Lord, asked me if I'd ever considered ordination. I hadn't but
I did. Faith, at that time, was not a problem: I believed all that I had
been told on the subject, both at home, at school and in church.
And I believed it earnestly. Perhaps undue weight in bringing me
to a favourable decision was the prospect of being able to give
all my views at length to a tame and quiescent audience, every week,
perhaps even oftener. Also there was a certain freedom and variety
about the way of life (not an early service *every* day) and there was
the genuine hope and indeed conceit that I could do some good
to the world. Then there was the language, the enormous richness
of the bible and other Anglican literature, and a clear sense of
direction. And the immense riches of church music as a part of

one's work. No reason either why my new profession should interfere with my delight in at least listening as an audience to more and more of the 'secular' music I knew and loved.

Again I was lucky: just as Annie Hunt and Dr Williams had come at exactly the right moment for me musically, so now there was the Rector of Bury, the friendly and intelligent Hugh Hornby (soon to be a Bishop), so enthused by my decision to join the church that he offered himself as a sort of private tutor. I could go every week and talk with him and ask him any questions I chose. This resulted in a great widening of my terms of reference but was also a great pleasure and privilege. More important, he gave me a profound sense of the meaning and reality of religion which I later lost, only with pain and regret.

I visited Germany for the opera again in 1938 with Dr. Williams, this time somewhat more aware of what was happening politically. This was due marginally to my increased age; partly to talking to our very good and very frightened Munich landlady, Fräulein Keim; and partly to my increased awareness of the logic of Christianity through my talks with Hugh Hornby. I now took, as I must, religion very seriously. And to me, if Christianity meant anything, it meant pacifism: and I delivered a sermon to this effect to a young person's meeting in Bury on the Sunday that war was declared.

Cambridge where I went to read theology in 1939 was a revelation: the whole world widened, and subjects that had been on the fringes of conversation in the North became the natural centre of discussion in Cambridge, and in a setting of wonderful beauty which began to open even my dull eyes. In music, where I had been so well brought up, there were still new things to be learnt and shared. In fact from the very beginning music (and girls) vied with theology for my time and dedication. If I loved King's Chapel it was more for the music of Boris Ord's choir (which in my second year I joined as a volunteer) and for its awesome architectural beauty than for its religious import.

Lots of secular concerts too, lots of friends, not all of them musicians or theologians but most of them interested in and appreciative of music. Many of these friendships continued into later life, and included Diccon Shaw, son of Martin and himself a very gifted and promising composer who wrote many songs for me to sing; Bobby Irvine, later a highly distinguished geriatric specialist, and John Graham, a classic who joined the RAF and after the war became a priest of the Church of England as well as being chief crossword compiler for the Guardian (Auricaria). Philip Radcliffe was a don at this time but, mainly I think owing to his quite extreme shyness, I did not really get to know him until my next visit to Cambridge in the market garden/Oppenheim period (see later) when I also studied with him for a while. Once the ice was broken he was a wonderful companion, very funny in anecdote and immensely knowledgeable in music. You had only to mention a piece of music, however obscure or fragmentary, and he would raise his hands and cry 'Ah!' and swoop on to his piano, saying, 'You mean this?' and play it off fluently with his peculiar long-fingered technique.

21

At first I tried to stifle my doubts about my vocation by forcing myself into ever greater fervency: in my second year I was even president of the King's Student Christian Movement. But in the end, my almost wilful and deliberate ignorance of the Hebrew language, in which I was required to sit a paper, ensured that I had to abandon my theological studies (I was later awarded a war degree) and I returned to music. I resolved to become a singer.

As it was wartime I had, of course, to perform some sort of community work compatible with my pacifism. The blitz had started and I moved to London and took up residence in Stepney at St George's Rectory (Hawksmoor's church next door had been an early victim of the bombing). The Reverend John Groser (famous for his rent marches in peace time) and his wife, had assembled there a group of scholars, dons, artists of various kinds, mainly pacifists. We helped and sometimes entertained local people, some of whom had been bombed out and others who went as they had done in the first

World War to shelter under the railway arches. I also had an organising job in the Control section headquarters of what was then known as the ARP, later Civil Defence. I managed to combine this for a period of about three months with a job in the chorus of the *Tales of Hoffmann*. On the morning of the 16th March 1942 I married Diana Clay and in the evening performed in the first night of my first West End production at the Strand Theatre conducted by Walter Susskind. This theatrical engagement was allowed by Stepney ARP on the understanding that I would come back immediately to Control if a raid occurred while I was on stage. This, miraculously, never happened.

The job at the Strand Theatre I owed to Madame Elena Gerhardt, who with her husband had got out of Germany promptly in 1933 and taken up residence in Hampstead. 'God' said Ernest Newman in the Sunday Times, 'no doubt could if he wished create a more wonderful fruit than the peach. So far he has not done so. Similarly he could no doubt if he wished create a greater Lieder singer than Elena Gerhardt. Similarly he has not done so yet.' I learnt (I think from the New Statesman) that she was now teaching in Hampstead and I wrote immediately and asked for an audition. She was very encouraging and I started work with her at once on a two-lesson-a-week basis, for which my parents paid in spite of their 'no' to the prospect of a musical career. These lessons revealed to me in depth the sixth great composer of my musical pantheon, the first five being Handel, Bach, Haydn, Mozart and Beethoven. Of course I learnt much about Schumann, about Wolf, about Brahms; but the main importance of my years with Gerhardt was the increase in my knowledge, understanding and appreciation of Schubert.

There was much music-making during the war, taking such forms as Myra Hess's National Gallery lunchtime concerts, which so many, including myself, attended. As Stephen Spender said, 'People felt that music, the ballet, poetry and painting were concerned with a seriousness of living and dying with which they themselves had suddenly been confronted.'

For me this was a time of meetings: Gerhardt provided opera classes for some of her pupils run by Dr Fritz Behrend, a refugee conductor from Germany, a good and gifted man. He and his wife made ends meet by taking lodgers, one of whom I met at tea one day. He was a violinist who had found it too much waste of time to come downstairs on every occasion that the sirens sounded and remained in his upper storey flat all day, practising. He was an ebullient young man called Norbert Brainin. The Amadeus quartet was not yet formed of course; so I did not foresee the immense gratitude which I in company with millions of others would owe to this man and his colleagues. I have sometimes thought since that perhaps all opera directors should be compelled to listen one night a week to this other, this extremely other, form of concentrated music-making.

One day I came into the Strand Theatre and heard someone practising or auditioning in a neighbouring room and was stopped in my tracks by the striking musicality of the unknown singer. The company was about to go on tour (obviously my ARP work prevented me from accompanying them); Susskind was auditioning for a new Hoffmann: the auditionee was Peter Pears, just back from America. He was successful. Next time I met him was in *Peter Grimes*.

Gerhardt sent me for extra coaching to Gerald Moore: I performed with him later at my first Wigmore recital in 1947. I always thought that Moore was at his best as an accompanist not of instrumentalists but of singers – a fragile breed to whom he gave unswerving support. I found that his sympathy was quite phenomenal for he sensed and even anticipated the slightest variation of dynamics and tempo.

One of Gerhardt's accompanists was a fine pianist who became a lifelong friend, Leonora Speyer. Leonora introduced me to Maria Donska who was, indisputably, the finest pianist I have ever known. I believe she gave her first recital around the age of seven (in Poland) and when she was 13 or 14 she went to study with Artur Schnabel in Berlin where she and Leonora met. They both came to live in Britain in the 30s after Hitler's rise to power. Throughout her adult life Maria was from time to time incapacitated by illnesses which hindered her career, as indeed did her refusal to play music which she thought (usually quite rightly) to be second-rate. I recall that her two London Beethoven cycles in the 50s were rapturously received, as were her many recitals up and down the country, as were her all too few recordings. She was also (rare for such a dominating soloist) a very fine accompanist and played for me on a number of occasions in Lieder recitals, where her sensitivity to her partner as well as to the music was acute. We also used to play (for fun, not public consumption) piano duet arrangements of Beethoven string quartets together, some of them fiendishly difficult but quite enlightening. (Later she played in various concerts for Kent Opera, her final performance being in a Beethoven piano trio in a concert for Kent Opera in 1988.)

My ARP work took me to Chelsea where we lived until my brother's death in 1943.

My brother Edward was six years older than me. At the age of seventeen he was articled to Slater, Heelis & Co, a firm of Manchester solicitors, and at the age of 22 became a solicitor himself. He must have been about 19 or 20 when he realised that the thing which he wanted to do more than anything in life was to be 'in the theatre' if not as an actor (and he thought it was probably already too late to go in that direction) then as a director or even as a manager. The later part of his legal studies was in London where he went to the theatre sometimes as often as three or four times a week. He was modest and unpretentious, of a fierce integrity and could also be very, very funny. He treated me as a coeval though this must have been extremely difficult at times; and he showed some suspicion of my religious intentions. His own pacifism (about which we knew nothing until the war was already there) grew naturally from a moral rather than a religious root. He was aware that two pacifists in the family (one, and that one an ordinand, was just tolerable) could spell the ruin of our father's business. He therefore went to his tribunal, was successful and then asked to be allowed to read a statement saying that for private reasons he wanted to be in the air force as a pilot. (The private reasons were that he felt if he had to be in the forces, then he chose to be in the most dangerous one.) His request was initially greeted with suspicion and refused and he was sent into the army; but he was a man of great determination and eventually he was transferred and allowed to take a post as navigator in a bomber. During one of his last leaves he came to see me in my dressing room at the Strand Theatre.

He was killed on his thirteenth or fourteenth mission.

The only one of his missions which he considered justifiable was the one on the rocket and flying bomb test centre of Peenemunde.

I was moved to land work (market gardening) in Oxford and it was there in 1944 that my first son was born in the Radcliffe Infirmary. His name, as I knew it would be, was Tristan. While I was in Oxford I met Hans Oppenheim, who had come over to England, I think with the Busches. He now ran the Dartington Hall Music Group and needed both a tenor and a bass for the vocal quartet which formed half of the group. I was invited to be the bass of the quartet and my friend from Cambridge days, Diccon Shaw, the tenor. Thelma Weekes was the soprano and Bruna Maclean the mezzo and later we were joined by the very young April Cantelo both as pianist and soprano. It was Oppenheim who introduced us and especially, I think, me to a composer with whom I'd previously had no dealings whatsoever: Monteverdi. When not digging potatoes I worked regularly with Oppenheim and the others: this work consisted mainly in the study of Bach and how to perform his cantatas and Passions and the exploration of this completely new world of Monteverdi, his madrigals and his operas. We soon all moved to Cambridge (I transferring to Magdalene market garden) and there performed, in addition to our studies, a variety of concerts and recitals in small churches and halls, culminating in a performance of music of various periods at the Arts

25

Theatre, Cambridge, on the last night of the war with the founder of
the Arts Theatre, J M Keynes, in the audience. But the climax of our
work at that time came a few weeks later in the Rudolf Steiner Hall
in Baker Street, London, in a performance of works by Monteverdi –
sections of his operas as well as a number of madrigals. We were none
of us well known apart from Oppenheim himself and so it must have
been the composer and the reviving interest in the composer that
were responsible for the long queue for seats stretching down Baker
Street when we arrived at the hall. I don't know what happened to
the Dartington Hall Music Group after that. I do know that it
couldn't pay anything approaching a living wage but its disappearance
was a source of great sadness and I am particularly grateful to Hans
Oppenheim for what he taught me personally.

Among those who attended the concert at the Rudolf Steiner
Hall were the young and enthusiastic Wilfrid Mellers and Walter
Goehr who was busy setting up a tour of Johann Strauss's *The Gipsy
Baron*, re-entitled for some unknown reason *A Melody of Love*. I got a
small part in this production and spent some weeks touring the
country with it and getting to know Walter Goehr better. He was
kind enough to lighten for me some of the ennui of touring by
accompanying me in various songs of Schubert, Wolf and Schumann
in the blank spaces of days we spent in unknown, and sometimes
uninviting, provincial towns.

This was the time when Britten burst on the world. I had
already heard some of his song cycles and had been to the second
performance of *Peter Grimes*. It appeared that in addition to all my
discoveries of the past, here was also strong musical hope for the
future.

There seemed however to be little financial hope for the future so
on the 11th December 1945 I went for an audition to Sadler's Wells,
fearing that I might get into the chorus, a thing I had vowed never to
do. However, *Peter Grimes* had been a very big success and was about
to be revived; and Edmund Donleavy, the Ned Keene, was unavailable

for the new season, not expecting it to happen. I was offered his part and a contract for the extremely modest sum of £8 per week (rising to £10 in the second season), which naturally I accepted.

So I became a principal of Sadler's Wells Opera Company. With every performance I grew to love *Peter Grimes* more. Britten himself was a constant presence, often standing at the side of the stage during performances and listening, listening. I shall always remember the vividness of the moment in the pub scene when Ned Keene sings 'Everybody's very quiet' and Peter emerges into his aria beginning 'Now the Great Bear and Pleiades': what was and remains a magical moment. Fine as it was then, with the years Peter's voice grew richer and fuller. However it was not until twenty years and three or four singing teachers later that he became the great singer that he finally was. And I believe it was the teacher, Lucy Manen, who gave him the lift over the last hurdle. His courage and determination to make that voice, as he did, the servant of his wonderfully musical mind was remarkable. He was at his best I believe in his fifties when he and Ben together became not only the best Britten interpreters but the best Schubert recitalists of our time.

It was during that Sadler's Wells season, too, that I learnt to value and love Verdi for the first time. My first Verdi role was Monterone in *Rigoletto* – an elderly part (as were many of my roles as a young singer), but I loved cursing Rigoletto on a high F, thus initiating the tragic series of events. One young part which I did play was Schaunard in *La Bohème*. Though this was an enjoyable rôle to play, it started me thinking that from an objective and musical point of view Puccini joined with Leoncavallo and Mascagni in the sad and slurpy decline from the great days of Italian opera. (I could never believe in any of the people in Puccini's works, despite his technical skill. When the hero in *Turandot* reaches a great crisis in his life and sings 'Nessun dorma' I don't find that an adequate response.)

Sadler's Wells was a good place to be at that time, fresh from its survival existence during the war, with some good singers led by Joan

Cross, who as Director of the company had also led it to the triumph of *Grimes* (in the face of a great deal of opposition from some of the company). There were singers of the quality of Roderick Jones, Anna Pollak, James Johnston, Rose Hill and Elizabeth Abercrombie – and of course Peter Pears himself; and James Robertson had returned from the RAF to conduct, though *Peter Grimes* remained in the hands of Reggie Goodall, the interpretation of whose circular arm movements was a skill in itself. We did Vaughan Williams' *Sir John in Love*, and the composer himself came to many rehearsals, saying from time to time to the conductor 'Please play that more quickly, I don't like that bit.' I also took part in *The Shepherds of the Delectable Mountains*, a self-contained excerpt from his *Pilgrim's Progress*.

Vaughan Williams was a great man and a humble; for many, many years the central pillar of English music; and he was always prepared to speak up boldly for younger composers including those whose way of working was quite different from his own and whose views in every respect differed from his – so long indeed as he was convinced of their musical integrity.

I did other parts at Sadler's Wells from the dashing Prince Miskir in Rimsky-Korsakov's *Snow Maiden* to the drunken gardener Antonio in *The Marriage of Figaro*. But I was restless, and when Robert Atkins offered me the part of Feste in the Open Air Theatre's *Twelfth Night* I managed to get out of the Sadler's Wells summer tour and went to Regent's Park instead. 1947 was a good summer and I think we took to the tent for a performance only once. Feste is probably the most difficult of all Shakespeare's clowns and way beyond my capabilities at that time; but I sang the songs well and was praised in the press and I learned something from watching both the mature and experienced Kynaston Reeves as Malvolio and George Merritt as Sir Toby; and the younger, fresh-from-drama-school Viola and Olivia – Christine Pollon and Patricia Kneale – finding their way with skill. Robert Atkins, whose deliberately measured diction all young actors loved to imitate, found that he and I shared an interest in Wagner and that a discussion of the

Meister went down particularly well with whisky after a performance.

My daughter Mariana was born on 3rd March 1947 and with two children I bethought me in a general sort of way of the financial hazards of an artistic career, as foretold by my father, and so went straight from Regent's Park to the choir of St Paul's Cathedral. This job provided a regular though small stipend and also allowed me to continue with solo engagements outside the cathedral so long as I did not put in deputies too often. But although nobody could claim that St Paul's was, or is, acoustically a good place to sing in, this cathedral job had unlooked for advantages of different kinds: all musical.

There were fourteen services per week: every choirman had two days (i.e. four services) off per week; and for all the week's services there was one three quarter hour rehearsal on Wednesday afternoons, in the crypt near Wellington's funeral carriage. This meant that having processed into the stalls, starting from the statue of Donne in his winding sheet, and having faced the pile of music in front of one, it was frequently interesting to make the acquaintance of the solos one was going to sing that morning or afternoon. These were often 'verse-anthems' in which sometimes the alto would do his bit, followed by the tenor, followed by the bass. I recall the occasion, but not alas the piece, in which for the first time I shared a verse-anthem with Alfred Deller. I had met him in the vestry, of course, before services and was aware of his reputation, but the sound of that voice coming from the other end of the same choir stall was so utterly magical and other-worldly that I was deeply shaken and only just recovered in time to take my own solo. It was not the voice alone but the phrasing and musical understanding which shone through every line. And it was not that I was unused to such voices: I had from my earliest choir days known the 'male alto' singer and some very good male altos there were, but this was something new. It was also through Alfred's singing that I began to learn what Purcell was all about. I had of course previously heard performances of 'Dido's Lament' and 'Fairest Isle' but this was different; and a new musical door flew open.

Not only for me. Alfred brought back the counter-tenor voice from the choir stall to the forefront of the international concert hall and stage. To do this required exceptional moral courage as well as exceptional talent: present day audiences would be astonished at the extent and violence of the resistance which this 'new' voice aroused among the prejudiced, the ignorant and the merely conventional. After one concert in Germany a member of the audience rushed up, saying, 'Mr Deller you must be eunuch!' 'I think the word you are seeking,' replied Alfred, 'is unique.'

Alfred's insight into the work of Dowland and the lutenists and composers of the baroque period were many and profound; but his work for Purcell constituted nothing less than a revelation and a revolution. Purcell had for the best part of 200 years been highly respected, little loved and rarely performed. Purcell wrote much fine instrumental music but his greatest achievements were in his vocal and dramatic works (despite some poor libretti). In the latter he used the instrumental accompaniment, including his favourite ground-bass, to give strength and purpose to his original and fluid vocal lines. He is a performer's composer par excellence – which is to say that while all composers suffer from bad performance, some, like Purcell and Monteverdi are destroyed by it. And the trick of making Purcell come alive had been lost during the 18th and 19th centuries, particularly after the emergence of the contralto voice in the early 19th century. By the 1930s there were people in England (and on the continent), including Purcell's successors, Benjamin Britten and Michael Tippett, who had come to understand him. But it was Alfred who first translated that understanding into action. Michael Tippett was invited by Canon Poole to come to Canterbury to hear Alfred, who was then a member of the cathedral choir. He came and in the choir school of the City of Canterbury (where Orlando Gibbons had died and was buried) Alfred sang for Tippett. In Tippett's words recalling the moment: 'It was in these evocative surroundings that I heard Alfred Deller sing Purcell's *Music for a While* ... for me in that moment the centuries rolled back.' It would be difficult to exaggerate his influence in this field on present day performers, instrumentalists as well as singers.

Alfred and I became and remained close friends until the appalling shock of his death in 1979.

Early in our acquaintance a question about Purcell arose which demanded scholarly resolution. 'The person you want to see', Alfred advised, 'is Walter Bergmann.' So I called on Dr Bergmann in his Hampstead home. My query would have taken about 15 minutes to solve. I stayed for supper and the evening. It was the first of what must have been hundreds of such evenings, discussing and performing music by Loewe (new to me), Schubert and Schumann as well as Purcell, Bach and Telemann (one of Walter specialities and one who came to play an increasing part in my own performing life). The late night journey back from Belsize Square was always full of the exhilaration of discoveries which I owed to him.

Walter had been a lawyer in pre-war Germany but was arrested and imprisoned by the Nazis for defending the Jewish firm of Huth in court. He was suddenly released (thanks to his wife Greta's bribery of a Gestapo officer) and given six weeks to get out of the country so he fled by train and boat to England in March 1939, followed by Greta and small daughter Erika just before war broke out. Walter arrived here with 10 marks and two suitcases – one filled with music (including the Purcell fantasias), a recorder and a flute.

He had studied piano and flute at the Leipzig Conservatoire and was a skilled performer on harpsichord and recorder. His German law qualification was no use in England so he determined to do what he had always wished to and became a full-time musician. On his release from internment on the Isle of Man in 1940 he began work as a packer with the publishers Schott & Co, eventually becoming one of their most distinguished editors. His work included collaborating with Michael Tippett on editions of Purcell – particularly the songs and odes.

His life appeared to be based on a simple premiss: that there is nothing in the world more important than music: that music is meant to give pleasure: and that the greater the music, the more profound the pleasure.

Walter also understood and loved language, primarily German literature; though his perceptiveness and delight in English literature might have astonished those who only knew his somewhat idiomatic handling of spoken English e.g. his habit of prefacing statements of strongly held opinions with the challenging words: 'It is so!' These opinions were based on hard-won knowledge and he gave of his knowledge and his insights (and not only to his friends) with a disinterested and gentle lavishness which sometimes, perversely, caused people to undervalue his contribution to the art he served. The truth is that his influence on music in this country was undoubtedly wide, deep and lasting, not least in the work he did for and with children, and in his immense influence on the teaching and playing of the recorder.

I believe that towards the end of his life he said that the best things he had ever done were a poem he wrote in a Gestapo cell and the Pastorale for recorder and counter-tenor which was Walter's ultimate tribute to Alfred's voice and artistry.

For the next ten years or so after 1949 it was a very mixed and multiple life for me: jobs in music clubs up and down the country; oratorios up and down the country; singing-teaching at such places as Morley College and Goldsmith's College; appearances with the Amphion Ensemble and the newly-formed Deller Consort (in this country and abroad); many highly original concerts created by Walter Bergmann, including Musical Pills to Purge Melancholy with Laura Sarti and Claire Walmesley, a Restoration revue with music by Purcell and others ('a fascinating delightful entertainment which blew all ill-humours away in gales of laughter' wrote Michael Tippett); Telemann's short opera *Pimpinone*; and a number of interesting concerts with Colin Davis and the Kalmar Orchestra. At the same time with the

help of Dr Bergmann in his position at Schotts, I began my career
as a translator of songs and operas; among the operas were Haydn's
The Burning House, Henze's *Boulevard Solitude* and, for the New Opera
Company, Werner Egk's *The Government Inspector* in which I also sang.
(This type of work interested me and translation of operas into
English became a central concern of mine a few years later).

Throughout this decade I performed regularly with the BBC
Third Programme music of various periods including solo Lieder
recitals, much work of the 16th and 17th centuries with Alfred Deller,
and operas such as Schubert's *Alfredo ed Estrella*, Monteverdi's *Orfeo*
and Gluck's *Iphigénie en Tauride* with Suzanne Danco as Iphigénie.

One of the most valued experiences, early in this period, was the
opportunity to appear with the English Opera Group. This was a
company founded by Benjamin Britten primarily to perform his own
works, and the repertoire was usually restricted to operas of a limited
size. The performances were seasonal: a new production normally
opened at Aldeburgh then toured at home and abroad. (Although
some of our aims and terms of reference were different, it was the
English Opera Group's qualities which later formed one of the
inspirations for Kent Opera's work.) The opera in which I sang,
The Beggar's Opera, had its premiere in Cambridge before travelling
throughout England and Holland. This was Britten's own arrangement
of Gay's original, a work that has tempted many composers, rich in
dialogue and in music from a wide variety of sources. Britten's settings
give unity and added beauty. Frequently, with, for example, his
'realisations' of Purcell, I have felt that his own musical personality
was too strong for the purpose and that he did violence (what one
might call an affectionate violence – but a violence nonetheless)
to composers he was dealing with; but here he got it just right with
a delicacy and subtlety that were pure delight. Tyrone Guthrie
produced, Peter Pears sang beautifully, Nancy Evans was his Polly and
Rose Hill appeared again from our Sadler's Wells days to do a
magnificent Lucy Locket.

33

But the greatest part of the tour for me was the experience of being conducted by Ben. I knew that he was one of the greatest conductors and could feel the results, but I could not precisely define the causes which, logically, I should have been able to as they were affecting what I did. In his accompanying at the piano, for instance, there was a certain subtle rubato – a thing quite different from the rubato as used by so many 'romantic' pianists which simply screams its presence at you. It is to do with shaping a phrase, making apparent the meaning and sense of a phrase by being 'unliteral' about the length of a note and its loudness in relation to the rest of the phrase. And as a conductor he could convey all that (with anticipation) to the performers. There exists a recording of Mozart's G minor symphony (among many others) which illustrates the fact that his gifts as a conductor were by no means restricted to performances of his own work. I once asked a distinguished instrumentalist who had played for every great conductor since the war to name the best. He chose Britten not just because of his gifts but because 'he made every performance a matter of life and death'.

In 1951 the Festival of Britain took place. This Festival, a hundred years on from that in the Crystal Palace, went from May to September. It was nationwide and planned six years after the end of the war, as 'an act of National reassessment and an affirmation of faith in the future'. The government, the LCC, the Arts Council and the BBC were all involved.

It was a wide collaboration intended to display the British contribution to the arts, science and industrial design and to produce simultaneously an atmosphere of achievement and delight.

Throughout Britain professional and amateur events, productions and festivities took place with an emphasis on performances and exhibitions featuring artists, living and dead, local to their area. And where festivals already existed they were incorporated.

In London where I lived there was a special eight week London Season of the Arts in May and June. The LCC filled its newly built

Royal Festival Hall with nightly concerts. And it decorated the South Bank space and buildings with commissioned murals and designs by Graham Sutherland, Victor Passmore and John Piper and sculptures by Henry Moore and Jacob Epstein.

The LCC was also responsible for the Battersea Pleasure Gardens – a fantasy of extravagant gaiety by the river, designed by John Piper and Osbert Lancaster with pavilions and arcades, towers and pagodas, lakes and fountains, restaurants and a tree-walk, two theatres and a miniature railway designed by Emmett of Punch. Not to mention a funfair.

Away from the South Bank the Arts Council was responsible financially for what went on during the richness of those eight weeks and their support was given to all branches of the arts.

Works of art in the public galleries that had been removed for safety during the war were now finally redisplayed often with an emphasis on special works in the collections – the Constables at the Victoria and Albert, the Turners and Blakes and a special Hogarth exhibition at the Tate. Most of the major commercial galleries also put on exhibitions.

In theatre there were special Festival of Britain productions. At the Old Vic, Shakespeare and Ben Jonson, Euripides and Chekov. At St James's Theatre there was old with new – Shakespeare's *Anthony and Cleopatra* and Shaw's *Caesar and Cleopatra* with Lawrence Olivier and Vivien Leigh. Elsewhere Alec Guiness played Hamlet and John Gielgud, Diana Wynyard and Flora Robson performed in Peter Brook's production of *A Winter's Tale*. There was a special ballet season at Sadler's Wells, including John Cranko's new work *Pineapple Poll* to Sullivan's music. Poetry readings were sponsored by eight major poets of that time, including Betjeman, de la Mare, Spender and Day Lewis.

Music, outside the Festival Hall spread out through London from the Royal Albert Hall to the Central Hall Westminster, from the Victoria and Albert Museum to the City churches. And it spread even more widely in a special BBC series of concerts whose artists included Pears, Britten, Deller and Joan Cross.

The stated Arts Council policy on opera was to use the Festival of Britain as 'a lever to help the good work on and see whether, when the festivities are over, our operatic health is sturdier as a result of the special effort.' It therefore coaxed new operas into existence, such as Vaughan Williams' completed *Pilgrim's Progress* and Arthur Benjamin's *A Tale of Two Cities* in which I sang.

At the Royal Opera House there was a Wagner season and the English Opera Group at the Lyric Hammersmith gave a Britten season that included *Albert Herring* and *Let's Make an Opera* plus Britten realisations of *Dido and Aeneas* and Monteverdi's *Tancredi and Clorinda*.

Summer 1951 was a good time to be in England, especially London, in the midst of so much imagination, creativity, enjoyment and faith in the future. Then the performing arts were considered central; 50 years later it was mainly entertainment technology with which we celebrated the beginning of a new century. And with the disaster of the 'what-shall-we-put-in-it?' Dome.

After *Twelfth Night* I had been eager to learn more about acting, especially of Shakespeare, and meeting the producer and librettist Eric Crozier in Regent Street one day I mentioned this to him. 'You should go and see Bertie Scott' he said emphatically. So for the next four years I did. Herbert Scott had been encouraged to come to England from Ireland by Tyrone Guthrie, and many of the celebrated actors and actresses of the day used him as their guide and mentor. He was enormously helpful to me. Then in 1953 I was invited by John Harrison (whom I had met on an Arts Council tour) to take the part of Amiens in his production of *As You Like It* at the Nottingham Playhouse of which he was director at the time. The music for the play was by my old Cambridge friend Diccon Shaw and it was in this production that I met Morris Perry at the start of his career. During our off-stage time we played endless games of chess together, all of which he won. In later years he appeared on a number of occasions for Kent Opera, speaking Donne and Shakespeare and others at concerts and assisting with advice on opera productions.

He has been the second person to teach me, mostly by example, skills that applied as much to singing opera as speaking Shakespeare.

In February 1959 my father died.

A year before, after a long period of chaos and unhappiness it seemed best, even for the two children, that Diana and I should separate. I vowed I would never marry again. All of which is of no interest to the general public except in that, after a few years, I met Johanna Bishop and broke that vow: and the interest to the general public is that without Johanna's help, commitment and confident imagination, Kent Opera would not have existed.

My whole life till now had been most fortunately full of music of every kind. And I had given a great deal of thought to the performance and meaning of music and in particular to its offshoot, opera. The difficulty of saying anything to the point about music is that it speaks its own, very precise language: which is to say that if it were possible to define its meaning in words it would be unnecessary to write music at all. But when we come to opera – and song – a new element is introduced: that of music's further ability to define character and personal emotions. When this 'dramatic' element is added you are faced with a potential richness of experience which is quite inexhaustible. And it is this very depth, breadth and richness offered by the great operas which renders them vulnerable to exploitation. Opera involves singing, acting, an orchestra, usually a chorus, sometimes dancers, a conductor, director, designer and a correspondingly large music, technical and stage staff: a standing invitation to megalomania and trivialisation. How to get the priorities right? How to fulfil the Chestertonian paradox:

'One thing is needful – Everything:
The rest is Vanity of Vanities.' ?

I felt I knew.

I felt that with the experience of nearly 40 years of music plus my missionary zeal I might be able to bring into existence an opera company that could achieve 'Everything'.

I had from the beginning certain clear ideas of what the company should be like. It should not be in London but in the musically deprived and neglected provinces. It should be seasonal for artistic even more than economic reasons. It should always put each opera's composer at its centre, with cast and orchestra of the intended size, never swollen or cut down. It should provide work of the highest quality without financial waste. It should have a main base (but not the terrible expense of an 'owned' theatre) from which productions should tour to other regions (including London). It should not be an operatic ghetto but should spill over into concerts, exhibitions, recitals (and of course education). Originally I envisaged a loose partnership with a theatre company on a repertory basis where each company could learn from the other and imaginative programming could be achieved. This unfortunately did not prove practical – repertory theatre companies were dying fast at the time.

There are so many wonderful things in opera and I wanted other people to share them. I knew what joy could be conveyed to audiences unused to having access to opera.

I knew what the repertoire of this company should be – it should have Mozart at its heart but should extend backwards as far as Monteverdi and forwards to specially commissioned works, taking in the best of both regular and little-known operas on the way. My only test would be quality. For instance no Mascagni or Puccini (whom I had outgrown at Sadler's Wells): but I hoped that such a company would one day mount Wagner's *Tristan and Isolde* with lyric voices (when it had access to a theatre with a big enough pit). The operas should be sung in English. And the ticket prices should be affordable.

I discussed my ideas frequently – so much so indeed that Johanna suggested in 1964 that it might be a good idea if instead of talking about it I did something about it. So I did.

I wrote to the Arts Council (who lost the first copy of my letter and plan). I wrote to theatrical and musical friends in different parts of the country outlining the sort of thing I had in mind; and there was for a period the possibility that Kent Opera might have been Bristol Opera or Birmingham Opera.

Meanwhile, in Kent, Alfred Deller had recently created the Stour Music Festival: a particularly original and imaginative project at that time of few festivals, which involved using fellow musicians from here and abroad, to play mainly music by Purcell, Bach, Handel and the Elizabethans. In the early years artists such as Nicholas Harnoncourt and the Concentus Musicus, Gustav Leonhardt, Franz Brueggen, David Munrow and Robert Spenser performed. In addition Alfred included chamber works by living composers such as Tippett, Ridout and Rubbra, while the centrepiece, given by the Deller Consort, with whom I performed, was a work such as *The Masque of Alfred, The Fairie Queene* or *L'Amfiparnaso*. These works were performed in beautiful and appropriate settings in the Stour Valley, such as the elegant house and gardens of Olantigh, or the fine churches of Boughton Aluph and Wye. The artist, John Ward, organised exhibitions, illustrated the programmes memorably, created the Stour motif – a drawing of a musical statue from the Olantigh garden – while Alfred's wife Peggy, a painter herself, acted as honorary secretary and provided warm hospitality to musicians and friends.

Alfred was eager to extend high-quality performances of music in the county so when I explained my opera plan he said firmly that if this company was going to be anywhere it was going to be in Kent and that he would produce a back-up of influential friends to form a committee to ensure that it happened. My view was that the first place to come up with practical support deserved the reward. So Kent it was.

creation

It is the glory and good of Art
That Art remains the one way possible
Of speaking truth.

The Ring and the Book Browning

Kent Opera

This is not simply the story of the concept and successful
development of one company followed after twenty years of valuable
creative work, by its destruction: it is, in combination with the next
two sections, a Morality Tale about the Arts, especially the Performing
Arts in England.

Kent Opera was founded in 1969 in response to a perceived need
and an idea. The 'need' was for people throughout England to have
first-class opera regularly available; the 'idea' was to provide it with
productions that should be composer-centred.

At that time the English regions depended operatically on
occasional flying visits from London (to eg. Manchester) and small
cut-down versions with piano accompaniment from companies such
as The Opera Players. Scottish Opera and the Welsh National were
both emerging (the latter at first depending on an enthusiastic amateur
chorus), but regular English opera companies on a regional basis
outside London were looked upon officially as impractical and
unnecessary, unwanted. (Opera North of course did not then exist.)
My experiences from Bury to Bayreuth told me that this view was

Pembles Cross Oast House, Egerton: the office of Kent Opera 1969–1989 wrong; that opera was not just an expensive frivolous pastime unconnected with 'real music'; and that there were still many valuable steps to be taken along the path initiated by Lillian Bayliss at the Old Vic and Sadler's Wells: this time outside the capital.

When I came to look at the spaces available in Canterbury and other Kent towns we had problems. (These were not, in fact, unlike the conditions Britten faced in Aldeburgh when he started his Festival there and before he converted the Maltings.) The great city of Canterbury had its promisingly named Marlowe Theatre to welcome us: this was a converted cinema holding 600 or 700 with a small orchestra pit which could be extended by removing members of the audience; no chorus room or green room, few dressing rooms and a minute wing space which meant that if you exited right, the only way to enter again left was by walking round, rain or no rain, through the car park. Tunbridge Wells had the Assembly Hall, a larger, grander and uglier theatre very suitable for wrestling bouts, for which it was much used; it had no orchestra pit and few dressing rooms. There was (and still is) a beautiful old (1875) theatre in Margate that was being used as a bingo hall; it was capable of holding 600 to 700 but had no dressing rooms and a general shortage of facilities. (Kent Opera managed to go there once, much later, for performances of a production in 1997 of Monteverdi's *Orfeo*.) After Kent Opera started, Dartford bravely built its own theatre and consulted us about the orchestra pit; the Assembly Hall put in raked seating; and Canterbury City Council at last, in the 1980s, made a move towards getting a better theatre for the city – a conversion of a larger cinema – and in consultation with us built on a good sized stage, new dressing rooms and a pit. Roger Butlin was asked to redesign the auditorium: a fearsome task that he achieved with success and subtlety, softening the rather bleak length of the building with the colours of a skyscape – seats in graded shades of blue, and sky and clouds on the walls.

It was soon obvious that Kent alone could not provide an adequate outlet for the kind and quality of production I intended to

mount and did in fact mount. Within a decade there was scarcely an
area of England which Kent Opera had not visited and within this
wider span gradually emerged our own home area spreading mainly
across the South of England as far west as Plymouth and covering
East Anglia, including Norwich and Cambridge.

In addition, during those ten years, having opened at Canterbury
and Tunbridge Wells with Monteverdi's *The Coronation of Poppea* in
1969; Kent Opera visited its first Festival (at Hintlesham) with
Handel's *Atalanta* in 1970; presented its first commission, Alan Ridout's
The Pardoner's Tale, in 1971 (with Alfred Deller singing the part of
Death); made its first foreign visit (to Portugal – Lisbon and Oporto)
with a fuller and truer version of *The Coronation of Poppea* in 1974;
gave its first prom with the same work in 1975; was invited to
Schwetzingen with a double bill of *The Pardoner's Tale* and Blow's
Venus and Adonis in 1976; and to the Edinburgh Festival with

The Pardoner's Tale Ridout (1977) with Alfred Deller as Death, David Johnston as Mean,
Graham Nicholls as Gross and Neil Howlett as Young

Gluck's *Iphigenia in Tauris* and Verdi's *La Traviata* in 1979.

But these special events, like the numerous broadcasts, were simply the prestigious offshoots of the main work, which was: to present the best performances of the best operas of all periods in our appointed area and to find the best people to perform in them for a chosen period with a guarantee of consistency of quality and an absence of waste in production or administration. And the success of the company demonstrated that the 'need' which we had foretold did in fact exist.

Opera is an almost impossibly demanding art form. But it can work if the priorities and purposes of the company are right, and the first priority is that the company should be run by a musician. Our ballet companies are run by dancers; our theatre companies are run by actors or directors; our opera companies are run by executives who may be fond of music. If you're going to run a market garden you don't get someone who's fond of lettuces because you'll get a rabbit.

The occasions when a musician has been in charge of an opera company have been few but memorable.

The opening of Glyndebourne (1934) profited from the arrival in this country from Nazi Germany of Fritz Busch and Karl Ebert who ran the artistic policy of the company until the war as well as conducting and directing. There was a brief period when Sadler's Wells was run by the singer Joan Cross (without whom we might not have had *Peter Grimes*) and of course there was the English Opera Group, run by Britten himself.

For the rest, the companies in 1969 (and now) were in the charge of 'managers' with no direct knowledge or understanding of the musical or dramatic needs or even of the financial priorities of an opera company. We have seen some of the results of this in recent years, especially at Covent Garden.

To start as one must with the music:

I had been looking for a suitable conductor for the future

company for some time when I met Roger Norrington, who was conducting a performance in South Kensington of *Noye's Fludde*, in which I was singing the part of Noah. Here, I thought, was a possible answer to my search and I asked him to take part in experimental performances of Purcell and Telemann operas which I was putting on with Walter Bergmann in Worcester and Exeter. On the strength of these I booked him for the opening of Kent Opera and then (as Roger himself said) kept asking him back for one production after another. I always tried to push other people forward; it didn't take much skill or effort with Roger. Until he came to Kent, Roger had had little experience of opera, which made it all the more remarkable that during the first ten years he conducted some of the best performances of Mozart and Verdi and Monteverdi – a very contrasting group – that I have ever heard.

The orchestra was, at first, the Midland Sinfonia (later I believe it changed its name to the English Sinfonia). But after about two years, as the number of our performances increased, it was obviously impracticable to employ a named orchestra with its own programme to fulfil; and what we were looking for, with our wide repertoire, was an orchestra of our own which was at once more flexible and more consistent. I think the management and achievement of these apparently contradictory aims was mainly the work of our two successive orchestra managers (both viola players): Colin Kitching and Nicholas Logie.

They chose the orchestra from freelance players, largely soloists whom they already knew from their own playing work or whom they auditioned. This produced instrumentalists very different from the usual orchestral players. Total commitment was required and given. The result was an orchestra of 'versatile and virtuoso instrumentalists' (*Daily Telegraph*), most of whom returned to play with the company season after season.

When Ivan Fischer joined us to conduct *Agrippina* in 1982 he commented on how I always gave a very special importance to the orchestra, much more than other opera administrators. 'It always gives me tremendous joy to come back to Kent' he said. He also pointed out one of the advantages of touring when the company rehearses before most performances. 'So the orchestra is now used to the idea that after a premiere it is the most natural thing for the production to be polished until the last performance. This is unique, and one of the things that makes it one of the best chamber orchestras of all – not just in opera.'

By 1974 there were usually three operas in the repertoire at any one time (varying in the size of orchestra they demanded as well as in style) consisting of, say, a Monteverdi opera, a Mozart opera and a 20th century opera. Most of our players were experienced in different periods and fields of work and could play for all the repertoire (with sometimes a change of instrument). The company rule was that for every performance of every single opera and every rehearsal of that

Ivan Fischer with the Orchestra during a rehearsal of *The Magic Flute*, Cheltenham, 1987

work there must be no change in personnel. As with the cast and the chorus the orchestra must be identical at every performance. This may seem obvious but is not usual in a system that allows for deputies. It worked partly because, from choice, we did not perform all the year round but in fixed seasons (two a year).

I shouldn't imagine that there are many freelance soloists and chamber music players who would be happy to sit in an opera pit night after night all the year round. For our players the limited seasons could be an interesting and valuable part of their musical experience. At any rate it worked. And we were most fortunate in our three main leaders over the 20 years, John Holloway then Paul Barritt followed by Susie Mészáros. I think we found out gradually that the ideal number of performances per year would be about 60 odd plus festivals and visits abroad and concerts. And Kent Opera was praised, not only in the press, not only by Ivan, but generally, as having the best pit orchestra in the country.

Singers. Too many singers sing by superstition and the teaching of singing is very haphazard. What we demand of singers is to make a noise as secure as a first class instrumentalist and to think like an actor, which seldom happens.

From the 17th century until the beginning of the 20th there existed in the West an art known as 'singing', a trick or method carefully learnt to do justice to the music to be performed, an accuracy and certainty of technique demanded nowadays of instrumentalists. Not, of course, that all the singers of those past centuries attained the highest possible standards but there was at least a norm of what was understood to constitute good singing by which performers could be judged. (And traces of it can still be found underneath the scrapes and scratches of old gramophone records made towards the end of the 19th century). Today that norm, sometimes known as 'bel canto', has disappeared because there was finally a reaction against what was seen as meaningless sound, but now, vocally, practically anything goes, from the shrieks and wobbles of 'heroic' drama at one end of the spectrum to the etiolated vibratoless murmur that is perpetrated in the name of 'baroque' at the other. Mozart, as usual, got it right not by writing a treatise on the subject but in a casual remark made to his father in a letter of 1778.

'Meisner, as you know, has the bad habit of making his voice tremble at times, turning a note that should be sustained into distinct crochets or even quavers – and this I never could endure in him. And really it is a detestable habit and one which is quite contrary to nature. The human voice trembles naturally – but in its own way – and only to such a degree that the effect is beautiful. Such is the nature of the voice; and people imitate it not only on wind instruments but on string instruments too.'

There are of course a number of gifted vocalists who have found their way through the confused standards now rampant (wobbling,

shouting, not thinking of the meaning, poor phrasing); but one has to look for them.

Many of the soloists we found such as Thomas Hemsley, Rosalind Plowright, Anne Pashley and Jill Gomez were well established; John Tomlinson had sung small parts at Glyndebourne, whence also came Enid Hartle who took part in so many of our productions; when Lynne Dawson sang Countess Almaviva in 1985 she was at the beginning of her operatic career. Our extensive auditions produced some discoveries. Sarah Walker was already known as a young concert singer but made her stage debut

Agrippina Handel (1985) with Felicity Palmer as Agrippina

The Return of Ulysses Monteverdi (1978) with Neil Jenkins as Ulysses and
Sarah Walker as Penelope

with us as Ottavia in our first production of Monteverdi's *The Coronation of Poppea*; later, at the Proms and elsewhere she took over the title role and went on to perform other leading roles with the company, perhaps most memorably she sang Penelope in Monteverdi's *The Return of Ulysses*. Felicity Palmer was a newcomer to the stage when she appeared for us as Dido; ten years later when she came back to us as Agrippina she was mistress of the stage, a subtle and strong actress. For Jonathan Summers, our first Rigoletto, we had to fight a three month battle against the Ministry of Employment (Summers was an Australian). We won. English National Opera and Covent Garden, who had watched to see how we got on, then snapped him up; but he returned to us as Orestes in Gluck's *Iphigenia* and Ford in Verdi's *Falstaff*. Gwion Thomas grew from the small part of Morales in *Carmen* to a wonderful performance as the leading character in *A Night at the Chinese Opera*. Also for *Rigoletto* we made one of our

The Barber of Seville Rossini (1985) with Eirian James as Rosina, Jacqueline Evill as Berta and Andrew Shore as Dr Bartolo

most outstanding discoveries: a very young Welsh soprano called
Meryl Drower as Gilda. She proved from the beginning to be a
remarkable actress as well as a fine and versatile singer and appeared
regularly with us. She was joined soon after by her compatriot, the
mezzo Eirian James, who also became one of our regular principals,
singing roles as various as Poppea, Dido, Cherubino and Rosina.

We were not a company in which you could make a career as
a chorister (i.e. receiving a regular annual salary) but when we
auditioned we were always on the lookout for a different type of
singer, one with solo potential who could be used (and therefore
paid more) as an understudy and also be involved in education
programmes. Several of our choristers have become soloists not only
with Kent Opera but in the wider world of opera and music as a
whole, for example Andrew Shore who, after giving perception and
wit to every chorus part he undertook, became a brilliant Bartolo in
our production of Rossini's *Barber* and thereafter has been a principal
with numerous opera companies here and abroad.

51

 Choruses need chorus masters and we were particularly fortunate
in this field with Jonathan Hinden, Timothy Dean and Mark Tatlow
who all combined this position with that of coach and assistant
conductor.

The director of an opera has a more restricted role than the director
in a play. In an opera all the main decisions have already been taken
by the composer and the composer's view of the drama as a whole
(much more than the librettist's) is decisive. Yet an opera is a dramatic
piece, a stage piece, and therefore we need a director as well as a
conductor: a director who together with the designer (and lighting
designer) will define the visual and active corollaries to the music.
The director should be (but rarely is) able to understand and therefore
to explain the dramatic significance of the music to the singers. If the
director is able to collaborate and take advice from the conductor

possibly all will be well. If not, not. Indeed all too often what happens in opera houses is that the director, working closely with the designer, has devised a plan of action and general imaginative and emotive approach to the piece before he has met the conductor. In Kent we were more fortunate. We did not have the experience of one company I was very reliably told about, where the director complained to the conductor that 'There's only music on these pages and no words so could we cut them out?'

I directed all the early productions as well as some of the later ones ; and both Roger Norrington and I were musicians so at least we both knew what each other was talking about and friction was reduced to a minimum. Our first guest producer in 1974 was Jonathan Miller, who was introduced to me by Roger and I was very doubtful because I thought nobody could do all the things that he did. And then I talked to him and I thought that to turn down that amount of

Cosi Fan Tutte Mozart (1985) with Margaret Cable as Dorabella, Patrick McGuigan as Alfonso, Neil Jenkins as Ferrando, Thomas Lawlor as Guglielmo and Elizabeth Ander as Fiordiligi

intelligence would be absolutely criminal. He then directed a wonderful *Cosi fan Tutte* for us. Jonathan was not a musician but his intelligence gave him the sense to listen to musical hints when made by musicians. He worked with us for some years, before other companies, here and abroad, woke up to his gifts and started employing him. In retrospect he wrote of Kent Opera: 'The clearest and strongest memory is that of intensely theatrical music-making and although I have done bigger things since with splashier names and more critical attention, I have never been involved with anything better. And I have a constant nagging suspicion that, as a producer, I was probably at my best.' I think that was true. I think we provided the basic, essential conditions of musical guidance, intelligent support and the strong company feeling in which he was free to use his brain, his imagination and his skill.

Jonathan is, as all the world knows, a marvellous talker and when preparing for his second production for us, *Rigoletto*, he spent many words convincing us that the piece belonged to the 19th century in which it was composed rather than the 16th century in which it purported to take place. All splendid stuff with which I heartily agreed. Then one night, in Eastbourne of all places, Jonathan started a fantasy about how the opera could be set in Al Capone's America; decor would consist of two bright car headlights shining from the back of the stage. All of which was very funny and we laughed heartily until a few mornings later Roger telephoned

Rigoletto Verdi (1985) with Jonathan Summers as Rigoletto and Meryl Drower as Gilda

me to say 'Jonathan means it!' I rang Jonathan immediately and he agreed to abandon prohibition America and return to his first concept, which turned out to be vocally and musically, dramatically and visually, one of our best productions.

He did, of course, a version of his American *Rigoletto* (but Godfather period) later for ENO in which, for example, his treatment of the dime-in-the-slot 'La donna e mobile' seemed to illustrate a director's misuse of music for the sake of an effect. He did however return to paths of virtue with his next production for us which was Monteverdi's *Orfeo*, a beautiful and musically aware piece of work.

Another producer whom we introduced to the general public was Nicholas Hytner. I had heard of him and seen something he directed at Cambridge. When I met him next he was a staff producer at the Coliseum. I thought it was a risk worth taking to offer him Britten's *The Turn of the Screw*. He was in his twenties, looked about eighteen

The Turn of the Screw Britten (1979) with Rebecca Platt as Flora, Sam Monck as Miles and Meryl Drower as the Governess

and also dripped with intelligence and awareness. He directed a fine and chilling production. He and Roger Norrington wanted a real child (not, as always before, a small adult) to sing the part of Flora; after auditions they chose my daughter Rebecca (then aged 12).

It was Hytner who wrote in Kent Opera's Twentieth Anniversary book his perceptive account of an opera director's relationship with an opera: 'Opera composers take extraordinary liberties with time and opera directors have to respond to the idea that the *motor* of the evening is music. In a play, the actors and director together will create the pace of a scene – where to pick it up, where to slow it down, what its *music* is. In an opera, the music is there, the pace is decided, and usually the scene moves in a totally unnaturalistic way. The actor asks '*What* is the pace?' the opera singer asks '*Why* is it paced like this?' To act an opera, you need to be able to think and move differently – sometimes slower, sometimes far bigger than life. And you have to know how to be still.' It couldn't have been said better.

Other directors who acknowledged the primacy of music in opera and who did fine productions for us were Robert Knights, Jonathan Hales, Adrian Slack and Adrian Noble, head of the RSC, who in his first venture into opera produced a strong new *Don Giovanni* with Peter Knapp in the title role, Janice Cairns as Donna Anna and Mark Curtis as her unusually convincing Don Ottavio.

So as a company I made sure we had little trouble with 'concept opera' where the director (and/or the designer) takes over from the composer as the main event of the evening; and in which he can say (I heard it said) 'Now what shall I do with this one?'

Set and costume designers were normally chosen by the director of a specific production after discussion with me and the conductor. Decisions on every aspect of production were made as far as possible by liaison with all the main people involved. And when the first designs were complete they were handed to the head of productions for costing to see if they fitted within the budget allowed.

As Kent was a touring company there were extra problems involved beyond choice of style and period – *Poppea* as Roman (the time of its setting) or 17th century (the time of its composition); decisions about the placing of rooms and doors (essential to the plot of *Figaro*); or how to convey a high mountain range in *A Night at the Chinese Opera*. These extra problems involved creating a set that would be large enough to fill the stage (less than 2ft narrower than Covent Garden) of the new Marlowe Theatre in Canterbury and yet still fit into the small space of the old Arts Theatre, Cambridge.

Occasionally there were disasters as when the square in Seville from *Carmen* proved impossible to squeeze into the Arts Theatre and was left leaning against an outside wall while the rest of the production went on inside the theatre. And then there was the dramatic occasion when Jonathan Miller's production of *Falstaff* hastened the refurbishment of the Theatre Royal, Bath by literally

Falstaff Verdi (1980) with Enid Hartle as Mistress Quickly and Thomas Hemsley as Falstaff

bringing the house down; for when the heavy Kent Opera lighting rig was put up, lumps of the ceiling started to fall on to a stage that was itself rotting. It was obviously too dangerous to perform on the stage area and it seemed that the evening's performance would have to be cancelled until Jonathan Summers, who was singing Ford, suggested the opera should go on minus set and lighting in front of the curtains. All members of the audience refused the offer of their money back and watched the show in its pared down state. Enid Hartle, who was singing Mistress Quickly, described the performance: 'The audience enjoyed the intimacy of having the singers almost in their laps and admired our courage when, as in the basket scene, we were in grave danger of falling into the pit and being impaled on a double bass. It was a memorable performance.' After this the theatre was closed for two years for a complete restoration.

Fortunately there were not too many performances memorable in this particular way, though at the Kings Theatre, Southsea, during another Miller production – *Eugene Onegin* – there were complaints from the singers that they didn't mind being rained on in the garden scene, but it was a bit much when the drops fell into Tatiana's bedroom. I believe the theatre roof was eventually repaired.

But to return to designers. Initially we spent most of our meagre finances on the musicians and singers, leaving it necessary to employ designers who could work miracles. And sometimes they did. In 1969 Nadine Bayliss solved the

Eugene Onegin Tchaikovsky (1977) with Peter Knapp as Onegin and Jill Gomez as Tatiana

Poppea problems of the changes of rooms in three different palaces with a series of moveable, marbled panels. Because of the inadequacy of the two Kent theatre fly towers these were designed to be slid, not flown – indeed throughout Kent Opera's 20 years most of our sets had to be basically free-standing. In our second year, 1970, Jean Jones created an enchanting wood for *Atalanta* out of trees whose leaves were made of orange transparencies which caught and glittered in the light. Simple, but most effective.

After a few years our increased (though still modest) grant from the Arts Council allowed me to allocate more money to sets and costumes and among the designers we used were Bernard Culshaw, Martyn Bainbridge, David Fielding and Roger Butlin. It was Jonathan Miller who introduced us to Bernard Culshaw who was fortunately able to react wonderfully to the stimulant of a limited budget and produced many splendid sets for us. I think he designed the sets and costumes for all the seven operas that Jonathan directed, including *Rigoletto* and *Falstaff*, as well as those for my own *Peter Grimes*.

I had known Roger Butlin before I started Kent Opera. He and I had worked together on opera productions when we were both teaching at Goldsmiths. Thereafter he disappeared among the stars, mostly American and Australian stars, and when he came back to the UK he found Kent Opera, approved of it, moved his home to Kent and has been close to Kent Opera ever since. His first design for me was in 1977 for Gluck's *Iphigenia in Tauris* (which we later took to the Edinburgh Festival). There was a beautiful neo-classical set on two levels – a marble floor on which the humans suffered and a luminous skyscape for heaven, storms and visions.

Richard Jones directed Judith Weir's *A Night at the Chinese Opera* of which the *Telegraph* wrote: 'A wonderfully ingenious production by Richard Jones and an equally brilliant permanent set by Richard Hudson. ... Nick Chelton's lighting is also a work of art.' Richard Jones described why he chose his designer: 'I realised that a highly versatile design was necessary. Apart from the problem of the changes in location … the design had to complement Judith Weir's musical aesthetic which is concise, lyrical, robust and very clear in its line. The solution arrived at with Richard Hudson pleased me because of its economy and wit which seems to me to reflect Judith Weir's intentions.' The set was a white box at the beginning of the period of fashionable white box sets, but the whiteness worked wonderfully for the snows of the Tat'ien mountains and the box was a box of tricks where a grave could open in the floor or planks be lifted to form ravines and narrow mountain ledges or a canal system could rise in co-ordination with the music.

Kent Opera was performing round the country to an audience that always included people who had never been to opera before. It was essential that everyone in the auditorium understood what was happening on the stage in front of them. Translation always loses

Iphigenia in Tauris Gluck (1977) with Eiddwen Harrhy as Iphigenia and Jonathan Summers as Orestes

something – the sound of the original language as set and fused with the music by the composer. Yet, more is lost when the audience cannot follow what is happening and the production has to distort, overplaying what needs to be understood. And it is also a matter of the singers; if you're going to sing meaningfully you've got to have all the reverberations of the language you are singing in and very few singers manage that. Instead they do good 'imitations' of foreign languages.

So we had new singing translations made for every opera. This is a highly skilled task where the words have to fit what the music is saying as well as fitting the notes; where if there is rhyme in the original, the English should also be in verse; where repetitions of half-lines need to make sense; where the mood of the words is decided by the mood of the aria and the whole is dictated by the music.

The translations were made on the assumption that the singers could make the words clear to the audience. Sometimes, where the libretto is verbally poor a translation can be an improvement on the original (I thought this was the case when I'd completed my English version of *Fidelio*.)

I did the first few translations myself, including *Poppea* and *The Patience of Socrates*, and then shared the task with two remarkable discoveries in this field. Anne Ridler was famous as a poet and I had enjoyed her work since her first volume of poetry came out in 1939; she was particularly gifted and aware of what was important for this task. She translated five operas: *Orfeo*, *Il Re Pastore*, *Il Ballo delle Ingrate*, *Ulysses* and *Agrippina*. Professor Michael Irwin of the University of Kent, translated no less than ten operas for us and was equally sensitive to the musical as well as the verbal needs of the form.

There are, I believe, devices called surtitles which can flash above the stage an approximate English version of what is being said or sung below in German, French, Russian. etc. A moment's thought will show that if you have to keep raising your eyes from the stage and your attention from the music there is NO CHANCE that you can absorb simultaneously the long musical message which the orchestra and singers are conveying. There are enough demands upon the concentration in opera already. When I was young and even more arrogant than I am now I used to think that audiences should learn the languages of the operas before they came; but ... When we went abroad of course we performed the operas in the original languages, for a foreign audience was more likely to have some acquaintance with the original than with an English version. Thus we performed *Poppea* in Italian in Portugal and *Fidelio* in German in Spain. In Singapore where English is the second language (as was evident from the detailed reaction of the audience) *Don Giovanni* was sung in English.

And so we come to the crux – what all these singers, orchestral players, directors, translators, designers, lighting designers (and the expert stage-staff backing them) are gathered together for: the repertoire. In the twenty years between Kent Opera's birth and its would-be murder (I say 'would be' since resurrections are quite common in the performing arts) we presented our audiences in this country and abroad with examples of most periods of opera composition: from Monteverdi's three great operas at the beginning to four 20th century British ones at the end (two Brittens, a Tippett and Judith Weir's amazing *A Night at the Chinese Opera*)

The opera form is almost exactly 400 years old and during that period has taken on many national and international emphases. It came of an Italian court practice in which 'gentlemen' (e.g. Busenello) wrote very good and skilful libretti then got professional musicians to set them to music; appropriate musical forms, madrigal and recitative being bound together in a continuous story; but once Monteverdi got his hands on the form in his first great opera, *Orfeo*, there has never been any question but that music is the dominating element in opera. It was therefore appropriate that Kent Opera's first production was Monteverdi's *Poppea*, which I had first encountered when I sang with Oppenheim in the Dartington Music Group in 1945.

The company performed *The Coronation of Poppea* three times – in seasons in 1969, 1974 and (in a new production by Jonathan Hales) in 1986.

The earliest manuscripts of *Poppea* that exist, consist of a voice line with words and a bass line for the continuo instruments which accompany all the drama. Only in the sinfonie and ritornelli before and between scenes is the music filled out harmonically. There is no indication of speeds, dynamics or phrasing and indeed not much evidence of what instruments Monteverdi wished to be used. So for each production very different decisions have to be made from when one is performing a nineteenth-century opera where the size of orchestra and number and type of individual instruments are all carefully specified.

In 1969 Roger Norrington chose to use the edition by Raymond Leppard which had been made a few years previously but by 1974 when we took the opera to Lisbon and then on tour in England he, together with the members of the Kent Opera continuo produced a realisation that was simpler and closer to Monteverdi's original manuscripts. In 1986 Ivan Fischer also realised the score himself with the same number of instruments (14\15) but with slight variations – eg: fewer violins and the addition of two recorders and a trumpet.

The difference between the 1969 music and the two later realisations was of course the type of sound – not just because of the smaller orchestra and the baroque instruments but because of the singers who now sang in the intended octave. This meant that among other changes of voice we now had not a tenor but a soprano Nero singing together with Poppea (in 1974 Anne Pashley with Sandra Browne and in 1986 Patricia Rosario with Eirian James). This meant that in the final duet (which, authentic or not, is breathtakingly beautiful) when the decadent and wilful emperor and his courtesan celebrate their union and triumph, their equal voices mingle and twine as if they were the aural equivalent of intertwining limbs.

The Coronation of Poppea Monteverdi (1974) with John Tomlinson as Seneca and Anne Pashley as Nero

This was probably the first time since the seventeenth century that this work was heard on stage as Monteverdi intended.

After Monteverdi, England was quick to pick up on the idea of opera and devised a native character for this new form. Purcell was the ideal successor to Monteverdi yet he only wrote one opera, the magnificent *Dido and Aeneas*, before death in its clodhopping way intervened. As well as this opera we staged Blow's *Venus and Adonis* (which we took to Schwetzingen and to the beautiful and ill-fated La Fenice in Venice).

After Purcell's death the English stage was overwhelmed by Handelian opera. Handel provided the Company with two operas for our repertoire, first the delightful *Atalanta* then, at a much later date, with one of our greatest successes – *Agrippina*. I was told of this work by Winton Dean, got hold of a score and knew at once that I had a piece of pure musical gold in my hand. It was written by a very young Handel before he came to England from working in Italy; it has much more variety of emotion than we usually associate with early 18th century opera and the music shows Handel at his greatest. We had a fine cast who could cope with the changes of mood from near-tragedy and deep tenderness to a humour that frequently bordered on farce.

I have already mentioned Felicity Palmer's performance; the part of Ottone, the only honourable character in the plot, was sung first by Paul Esswood and then in the revival by Michael Chance, in his first appearance with us. Cynthia Buchan sang the part of the mother-dominated and lascivious Nero and Meryl Drower the jewel-loving but ultimately faithful Poppea. It was directed by Christopher Bruce (of Ballet Rambert) and myself. Roger Butlin was responsible for the design, based on the asymmetric series of arches that are part of the Baptistry doors in Florence and which through the false perspective gave a sense of space and (with Nick Chelton's lighting) of radiance. Most important of all it marked the first appearance with Kent Opera of Ivan Fischer. I had been following his work for some years, since

(Previous page) **The Coronation of Poppea** Monteverdi (1986) with Christopher Gillett as Arnalta and Eirian James as Poppea

I saw him win the Rupert Foundation Competition for Young
Conductors in 1976 and I booked him for *Agrippina* in 1982. In this
opera particularly, I experienced what I had felt at Bayreuth all those
years ago when 'everything joined together to achieve a marvellous
unity'.

Also from the early 18th century (thanks to the guidance of
Walter Bergmann) came a splendid opera by Telemann, which I do
not remember to have heard or seen elsewhere. We produced it quite
early on in the company's career and I had hopes of it because of my
earlier association with his short opera *Pimpinone*. This was a long
opera called *The Patience of Socrates*, which has two very rare qualities –
musical wit and endless invention. It was performed among others
by the present-day Wotan, John Tomlinson, April Cantelo and Neil
Jenkins, with Thomas Lawlor as the bigamous Socrates.

Gluck's 'reform' of opera was represented by his *Iphigenia in Tauris*,

Unloading Kent Opera's scenery at La Fenice in Venice (1980)

which had struck me forcefully and favourably when I sang the part of Orestes in a broadcast some years before. I had a particularly strong cast with Eiddwen Harrhy as a passionate Iphigenia, Jonathan Summers as a subtle and tormented Orestes and Anthony Roden as his friend Pylades.

In addition to performing the rarely seen and heard *Il Re Pastore* (with Jill Gomez and Patricia Rosario), all the main Mozart operas appeared more than once in our tours, and rightly so as Mozart was, is, and as far as I can imagine ever shall be, the centre of the operatic repertoire. Let me explain.

If opera took its place among the arts in 1600 it reached its peak in the short period from 1786-1791. It was during this period that Mozart composed *The Marriage of Figaro, Don Giovanni* and *Cosi Fan Tutte*; and the very different *Magic Flute*. It would seem that the decisive factor in the composition of *Figaro* was the work of

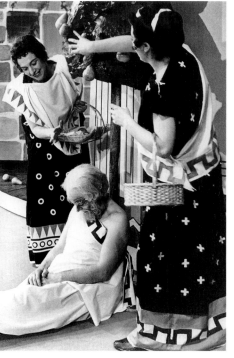

Beaumarchais in Paris, filtered through the words of the gifted librettist Da Ponte, whom Mozart met at this time. This influence is also more than obvious in the other two Italian operas. In the case of *The Magic Flute* the decisive factor was his fellow mason Schikaneder. Mozart also wrote, of course, in the last year of his life *La Clemenza di Tito*, full of wonderful music but seemingly unrelated to the human experience and awareness which he had displayed in the three Italian operas and to the wider philosophical sensitivity displayed in the German *Magic Flute*.

(Previous page) **Agrippina** Handel (1985) with Meryl Drower as Poppea and Paul Esswood as Ottone. (Above) **The Patience of Socrates** Telemann (1974) with April Cantelo as Xantippe, Thomas Lawlor as Socrates and Linda Esther Gray as Amitta

La Clemenza di Tito was of course a commission hurriedly undertaken (completed in three and a half weeks) under the pressure of a desperate need for money.

We are unlikely ever to know precisely what the relationship between Da Ponte and Mozart was and why it made such an enormous difference to Mozart's work. He had of course written very fine music for the stage throughout his teens and his early twenties but here was something, some extraordinarily subtle psychological awakening, which combined with his musical maturity to produce characterisation in music never witnessed before or since. It could be that the clue was given in his correspondence with his father: but we shall never know since Constanze destroyed his father's letters of this period after her husband's death.

I shall try to illustrate this – what shall we call it? – musico-psychological skill with two examples from *The Marriage of Figaro*; one

The Magic Flute Mozart (1987) with Patricia Rozario as Pamina and Mark Curtis as Monostatos

rather simple and obvious, the other somewhat more complicated. But it must be noted that in neither case is it a matter of using music to 'illustrate' words; such illustrations belong to the realm of the more obvious music-hall effects not to the delineation and gradual unfolding of character or the revelation of relationships.

So we take as our first example the beginning duet of the whole opera between Figaro and Susanna. Figaro is being practical, measuring and counting, trying to work out if their bed will fit into the new room that the Count has offered the engaged pair for their use after their marriage, ostensibly as an act of generosity. Figaro counts in sharp statements mainly in crotchets of the tonic and dominant; he is the practical man who is going to get things done. Susanna enters and tries to distract Figaro by displaying the new hat she is hoping to wear at her wedding that day. She sings in a long flowing tune of quavers; and so they argue in their own melodic language. But it is Susanna who wins and in whose tune they join at the end of the duet. And this sets a character pattern for the whole opera. For Susanna is in fact cleverer than Figaro who has not, for instance, noted the reason for the Count's 'generosity' in placing their bedroom so near his own. Her own superiority in wit is thus established musically before it is revealed verbally.

My second example is the famous finale of Act II. Mozart's symphonic experience and knowledge is the bedrock of this very extended piece. A list of the keys through which it passes is instructive. They are: E flat leading to B flat which is abruptly interrupted by the shock of the rather distant key of G (Figaro's entrance which nearly disrupts the whole scheme of the Countess and Susanna); the key of C followed by a whirling F (the drunken gardener's entrance) and so back inevitably to B flat and ultimately, with the arrival of three more characters, it returns boisterously to E flat, the original tonic of the movement. With the changes of key go changes of tempi and time signatures and the point is that these changes go hand in hand with dramatic development in which even

Don Giovanni Mozart (1983) with Geoffrey Moses as the Commendatore, Mark Curtis as Don Ottavio and Janice Cairns as Donna Anna

the interjections, interrupted sentences and exclamations seem simultaneously to be inevitable musically and to reflect the spontaneous dramatic timing of an actor. The key changes form a firm basis of development for an audience which does not even know what a key is: just as a concert audience accepts the finality of a final return to the tonic without necessarily realising the reason for this finality.

The great miracle is the fluidity of action and thought which Mozart musically conveys within these different sections of the finale. Nothing like it had ever been attempted or achieved before or equalled since. And this is why the lack of any detailed account of the working arrangements between Mozart and Da Ponte is particularly maddening. There is a tantalising letter from Mozart's father to Mozart's sister at this period which states that Mozart was having difficulty in getting the libretto into the order he wished. This does not of itself get us much further as Mozart always had difficulty with

The Seraglio Mozart (1984) with Eileen Hulse as Blonde, Harry Coghill as Osmin and Luce Garreau as the harem girl

his librettists. Whatever the trouble, this time the solution was more fruitful, perhaps simply because Da Ponte was more intelligent and responsible than Mozart's previous collaborators. The musical development of each section *appears* to be entirely a musical matter; yet the verbal and dramatic development seems to fit the music as though the words and the drama were the essential shaping factor; which is of course musically impossible. Did Da Ponte sit at Mozart's elbow and adapt his words on the spot to Mozart's requirements? Da Ponte was clever enough certainly; but it appears from his way of life that he is most unlikely to have been able to spare the time. Or did Mozart, having received from Da Ponte the magic hint – whatever that was – supply and adjust the words himself to fit his own musical intentions? He was also clever enough and this seems to be the most likely guess. The same sort of question (and answer) applies of course to *Don Giovanni* and *Cosi Fan Tutte*. *The Magic Flute* is a different matter and different influences were at work though Mozart's creative brain would not have forgotten whatever it was he had learnt during the Da Ponte period, despite the fact that he was writing a completely different kind of opera. For *The Magic Flute* was the first and greatest of the long succession of German operas.★

But before we leave Mozart and those amazing six years there is one example of combined music and drama which is rather different from those so far mentioned. It is not an ensemble, it is not a duet even; it is an aria – Susanna's most well known aria from the fourth act of *Figaro*: 'Deh vieni non tardar'. Susannah is in the garden and she knows that Figaro suspects her and is listening there in the darkness. She sings a recitative and an aria ostensibly addressed to the Count, with whom she has an assignation, but meant to be overheard by Figaro with whom she is furious for even daring to doubt her fidelity. The recitative is full of amorous clichés all slightly but subtly exaggerated. The aria itself is accompanied by wind and plucked strings: at least, the strings are plucked until three quarters of the way through. Then the plucked accompaniment turns to warm, bowed

---

★ *The Seraglio* was of course the first of Mozart's great operas to be written in German but in style it still owes most to the Italian tradition.

phrases as the vocal line shifts from mockery to genuine warmth as she directs her real love not to the Count but to the angry (and listening) Figaro. He, of course, filled with jealousy and rage does not notice the change. But we, the audience, do.

It is one of the great moments of opera: a character that has been established by music being given added depth and warmth by music in a way unique to music. It is, in fact, in itself a justification of the operatic form; and the reason why Mozart was the centre of Kent Opera's repertoire.

Kent Opera was, incidentally, the first British company to be invited to take Mozart (Nicholas Hytner's production of *The Marriage of Figaro* with Alan Watt, Meryl Drower, Alan Oke, Lynne Dawson and Eirian James, conducted by Ivan Fischer) to The Vienna Festival (in 1986) at the Theater an der Wien (where Beethoven's *Fidelio* was first performed). I think this production by Nick was even better than his *Turn of the Screw* or *King Priam*, fine as they were. You can't be clever with Mozart, you've got to be wise, and he was.

Coming to the 19th century, as well as Miller's splendid production of *Fidelio*, we put on performances of two Rossinis: *The Barber of Seville* and *Count Ory*, Tchaikovsky's *Eugene Onegin* (with Peter Knapp in the title role and Jill Gomez as Tatiana), Bizet's *Carmen* (directed by Robin Lefèvre) and, Offenbach's *Robinson Crusoe* – not to mention two Gilbert and Sullivans.

These last three bring us into contact with a new world, a different world, the world of what used to be called 'light music': the world of operetta. This world calls for another book which I do not propose to write. But perhaps it is worth remarking that while it is true that great music is needed to transform one's 'weltanschauung', operetta can cheer one up temporarily (a not entirely unworthy aim); and that in order to do this adequately it needs the skill and resources of a first-class opera company.

We performed three Verdi operas. Verdi in maturing developed subtlety of musical characterisation and drama in *Rigoletto* and *Traviata*

The Marriage of Figaro Mozart (1984) with Meryl Drower as Susanna, Lynne Dawson as Countess Almaviva and Alan Oke as Count Almaviva

and went on developing into his seventies, his freshness increasing with age, with *Aida*, the second version of *Boccanegra* and so on to *Othello* and, best of all, *Falstaff*. He was a man who never ceased to grow. Jonathan Miller directed his *Rigoletto* and *Traviata* and an outstanding *Falstaff* with Thomas Hemsley in the title role. In the 1980s I very much wanted to put on *Simone Boccanegra* but was prevented by shortage of money.

What of that other 19th century member of my original pantheon, Schubert? Why did Kent Opera never perform him? Perhaps the question should be: Why did Schubert, one of the most richly gifted, prolific and original of all composers, who virtually invented the song as a great musical form; who lived in Vienna at the same time as Beethoven whom he revered and of whom he stood in great awe and whose own compositions yet show complete independence of his fellow citizen; why did this man who could make character, situation and drama in the space of two pages never (despite many attempts) write a great opera?

Very few composers seem to have had the will or the strength to resist the power of the prevalent custom or fashion and to define and make their own terms of reference. The theatre automatically brings into play so many different situations and parameters (including the social) beyond those of music itself: conditions and disciplines of which the composer may have no experience whatsoever. Usually therefore he accepts the custom of the day and only gradually, if at all, turns away to assert his own ideas and needs. He is also usually dependent upon an already existing, quite considerable, organisation; he has to persuade this organisation that his new work will justify the labour and expense of mounting, preparing and presenting it. Schubert tried to fit in with many already existing forms (some nonsensical) none of which suited him.

Verdi and Wagner were both 15 when Schubert died. They had the time and firepower to produce each his own revolution. Not Schubert. If Verdi and Wagner had died at the age of 31 as

Schubert did, we should never have heard of them.

Schubert left evidence of some nine or more attempts at opera, some complete, some merely fragments. Of these the short Singspiel *Die Verschworenen* (the Conspirators), changed by the nervous Viennese censors to *Das Häusliche Krieg* (Domestic Strife), is a slight but attractive version of the Lysistrata story and is one which Kent Opera might, given time, have brought into its repertoire. Despite Abbado's splendid advocacy for *Fierrabras*, the inanity of the story mitigates against its success.

If Schubert had met his own Da Ponte how different the history of opera might have been.

It was not until the 20th century that Britain at last took up Purcell's initiative of 300 years before, and towards the end of its 20 years Kent Opera performed several modern works including Britten's *The Turn of the Screw*, *The Burning Fiery Furnace* (which, like *The Beggar's Opera*, we took to the Aldeburgh Festival) and Tippett's *King Priam* as well as in 1987 Judith Weir's *A Night at the Chinese Opera*. The commissioning of Weir's work with its overtones of the Marx Brothers in the title and its tragic story that simultaneously provoked laughter was one of Kent's most significant acts for I believe it to be one of the great operas of the 20th century.

How did it come about? Robin Jessel, our finance director, had lent me a tape of Judith's *King Harald's Saga*, a Grand Opera In Three Acts For Solo Soprano Singing Eight Roles. I was immediately taken by its originality and by the combination, musically and verbally of tragedy and wit. (Like Wagner Judith always writes her own words, though hers are fewer and funnier.) I listened to more of her music, met her, and commissioned her (with funds from the Arts Council) to write a young people's opera for performance by a secondary modern school in Canterbury. The opera she wrote, *The Black Spider*, used the collision of two plots and the dislocation of time, jumping back and forth between a Polish legend of the Middle Ages and a recent newspaper cutting about a curse on the opening of a tomb in Cracow Cathedral. The piece was good enough to convert eventually even the most sceptical of the children who stopped saying to the producer, Amanda Knott, 'Don't want to be in your opera, Miss,' and instead said 'Our opera's great, Miss.' The opera's villain was sung by a Kent Opera tenor, Armistead Wilkinson; the rest of the work was written so skilfully for singers and an eclectic group of instrumentalists that the students were finally able to perform it most convincingly and to eerie effect in the crypt of Canterbury Cathedral.

The BBC at this time wished to commission a full length opera from us so I proposed Judith Weir as the composer. The proposal was accepted by Robert Ponsonby, the controller of music at the BBC, and I invited Andrew Parrott to be the work's conductor. The subject Judith chose for her libretto was China at the time of the 13th century Mongol invasion but it was a subject with strong resonances through

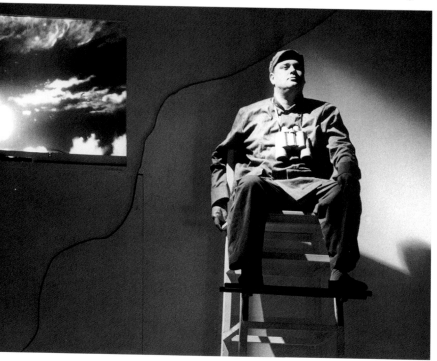

A Night at the Chinese Opera Judith Weir (1987) with Tomos Ellis as the Nightwatchman

history. It begins as the forces of Khubilai Khan climb over the city wall of Loyan while the Chinese night watchman is looking keenly in the wrong direction. A Chinese boy, Chao Lin, whose mother is dead and whose father was forced to flee to the Tat'ien mountains and his death, by the Mongol military administration, is brought up under Mongol influence, becomes an engineer and in effect a collaborator. In the central act of three, Chao Lin (Gwion Thomas) watches a performance by a banned trio of Chinese actors of an actual Chinese dissident play of the period – The Poor Orphan of the Chao Family – and sees that the story of the fictional boy orphan (Meryl Drower) echoes his own life. The performance is interrupted before the end but Chao Lin is now inspired to avenge his father and his nation by killing the Mongol military governor (Michael Chance). However, because of his own nature, Chao Lin can only attempt, not carry out the deed – he is prevented and arrested. In the final scene the military governor sits as a judge above the stage; four Chinese citizens stand before the place of execution; the actors complete their play to its happy conclusion while Chao Lin kneels, the executioner's sword falls, the lights go out and the music ends abruptly.

81

The libretto and music move seamlessly between comedy and tragedy and the music subtly incorporates Chinese musical influences into a 20th century masterpiece.

Judith spoke at the time of her collaboration with the company: 'It is very important to me to feel that I am writing music for particular people and sending it to them personally. Kent Opera is unique among companies for the way it works, having a musician as its artistic director, so that I am able to consult and be consulted, so that I can ring up and discuss the range of voices with Norman Platt; or I can contact Nick Logie, the orchestra manager, for advice and feel the close involvement of the whole company of musicians. In my short working lifetime I have seen the complete take-over of musical organisations in Britain by an administrative sector comprising people whose background is very rarely that of a professional musician; and

the results (particularly the inordinately large proportion of arts subsidies spent on administrative costs) cause me great concern.'

My final production for the company in 1989 was *Peter Grimes* – 43 years after my own appearance as Ned Keane in that first production at Sadler's Wells. Then Britten had been there for almost every performance. He said he thought the work had broken the ice for opera in England – which was rather an understatement.

From a director's point of view, the challenge of the work is in capturing its claustrophobia. Britten was keen to emphasise the claustrophobia of the community and the question is how to achieve this. The problem is you have to have the sea somehow, and it is vast, wide, deep, whereas the village community is very narrow and enclosed. In the first production all the village buildings were on stage and there was little space for the sea. Together with my designer, Bernard Culshaw, I tried to get the claustrophobia from the people, keeping the space for the sea and implying the buildings rather than stating them.

It is very much an ensemble opera with the principals playing their musically individualised parts yet merging with the chorus at such times as when the villagers go about their morning work or when they seek drink and shelter in the pub or become a terrifying mob in the hunt for Grimes. And the principals in this production, many of whom had appeared regularly with Kent Opera, could sing the demanding lines with ease and musicianship and act together to create the borough. They included Rodney MacCann (Balstrode), Meryl Drower (Ellen), Richard Suart (Swallow), Alexandra Mercer (Mrs Sedley) and Gwion Thomas (Ned Keane) to mention only half of the dozen excellent soloists.

And Peter Grimes himself? He is the outsider in the opera, one who does not fit in with the rest of the community, who is more ambitious, more passionate and angry, more visionary than the rest of the gossiping, close-knit villagers. The 'outsider' can be a metaphor for many types of individual. In this production the part was sung by

(Previous page) **Peter Grimes** Britten (1989) with Howard Haskin as Peter Grimes and Gwion Thomas as Ned Keane

Howard Haskin, who had already sung for us a passionate Don José
in *Carmen* as well as Paris in *King Priam*. His characterisation reached
a most moving and convincing climax in his mad scene against the
background of the off stage manhunt.

Ivan Fischer, soon, I thought, to be my successor as Kent Opera's
artistic director, conducted. I was (almost) content. And so was
Rodney Milnes who wrote in the Financial Times: 'This Grimes must
in its sheer immediacy reproduce the impact of that great night at
Sadler's Wells forty four years ago and that is saying something.'

So, over the twenty years, Kent Opera produced works ranging from
the birth of opera in early 17th century Italy to the rebirth in 20th
century Britain. It was not an easy time to be continuously involved
in the pursuit of excellence by mounting performances of this
potentially magnificent and notoriously treacherous form of art.
It was the time of relativism and the ironing out of values. It was
difficult to keep one's nerve when all around operas were being
chosen and produced not for their musical/dramatic quality but for
the opportunity they gave to ambitious directors and designers to
draw irrelevant attention to themselves. But I am sure that the realised
'idea' of producing the best operas according to the composer's
demands was the correct answer to the original perceived 'need'.
And the need was to introduce opera to the wide range of people
deprived or ignorant of its delight.

Kent Opera plus

The reason for the creation of Kent Opera was my conviction that
the arts are a human necessity. So opera was mounted across a broad
swathe of the country where previously it had not been available. And
the audiences had come. Still many, adults as well as young people and
children, were unaware of what had arrived on their doorsteps. We
therefore did two things: first of all we developed work with children
in schools; then we developed a programme of extra events for adults
– concerts, talks, exhibitions and poetry readings.

Already in the second year I had commissioned and put on Alan
Ridout's children's opera *Angelo* (based on Quentin Blake's story).
Then in 1981 I created an Education Department, the first opera
company to do so (two years before the Arts Council made it
mandatory). Carole Patey was the first Education Officer, coming
to the company from the Victoria and Albert Museum with a
background that combined teaching, music, writing and the visual
arts. In her six years with Kent Opera she initiated a stimulating and
highly enjoyable series of programmes directed at very varied age
groups. She did this in collaboration with Mark Tatlow, our head of

At the British Museum, exploring the Egyptian connection in Mozart's *The Magic Flute*

music for many years, and using the talents of singers in the company. In the final two years Johanna, who had previously contributed various writings and libretti, took over as Education Officer.

Many of the early projects were concerned to place opera in the context of other disciplines. Carole Patey began our association with the British Museum Education Service where, with the help of John Reeve and Patsy Vanags, operas such as *King Priam*, *The Magic Flute* or *A Night at the Chinese Opera* were set in the context of history, vase painting, Egyptian statuary or Chinese porcelain. Many projects placed music in settings that matched it – 18th century music was played in 18th century houses; *Bastien and Bastienne* was performed at Strawberry Hill.

I was always anxious to find new ways of exploiting the many-sidedness of opera and so in 1985, with the encouragement and financial help of South East Arts and after reducing the large number of applications to six, we finally chose Jane Lewis as the Company's Artist in Residence. I don't believe she had ever been to an opera before she took the post but she came to love the form and to find it a fertile source for her work. She was with Kent Opera for a year, producing paintings, drawings and a set of etchings, all of which were gathered into an exhibition which toured with the company's repertoire of *Agrippina*, *The Barber of Seville* and *King Priam*. We also used her work in our publicity material. In Kent Opera's final year of 1989 she produced three images for the operas *Fidelio*, *Ulysses* and *Peter Grimes* to be used as posters and programme covers. In 1989 also, John Ward (from the first a generous supporter) produced a painting of *Peter Grimes* (now in the Canterbury Art Gallery) that was made into prints for public sale.

Programmes based on operas in the repertoire were written and produced for all age groups. Some included specially arranged overtures for the children to perform. When *A Night at the Chinese Opera* was on the road, the composer led a series of workshops in which pupils created their own piece of music-theatre based on Chinese Yuan drama, the source Judith Weir had used. A film and music project, based on the theme of *Ulysses*, was organised in schools throughout our touring area; and in 1989 Michael Irwin wrote a play based on Rossini's life and *The Barber of Seville* for Junior schools.

Kent Opera's two main assistant producers, Amanda Knott and Mary Forey (both dancers) were much involved in the education programmes, particularly in directing the specially commissioned schools operas. These were set up in the belief that one of the most valuable forms of education is participation. Ridout's *Angelo* was followed in 1984 by Adrian Cruft's *Dr Syn*, a three-act opera for senior schools on the subject of the 18th century smugglers on the Kent marshes, and in 1985 by Judith Weir's opera, *The Black Spider*. In 1988, the anniversary of the Armada and the Glorious Revolution, Christopher Brown composed a pageant opera for Northampton children called *The Two Lockets* (directed by Patrick Young) which involved the students, their teachers, their parents and their friends.

(Six weeks later when the company visited Northampton there were large groups of children who had taken part, at every one of our performances of *Don Giovanni*, *Fidelio* and *Count Ory*). In the 1990s Ruth Byrchmore wrote a nativity opera for primary schools and *Baba Yaga*, an opera for tenor witch and 50 students.

Dr Syn was performed again as a community opera. Sometimes these productions had quite startling practical effects as when, for example, Paul Wallis, under the influence of singing in *Dr Syn*, transferred from washing-up in a pub to studying theatre design and then working professionally in the theatre.

Finally we tried to break down the purely artificial barrier

Dr Syn Adrian Cruft (1996) Community Opera in Ashford, Kent

between extra events (attended by adults) and educational events (attended by children). We encouraged students to join the adults at the open days, chamber concerts, poetry readings and song recitals and made certain programmes created for students available to the general public as well as schools – programmes such as *Fidelio – Prisoners of Conscience* (an interweaving of the themes of *Fidelio* with the writings of the wives of three 20th century political prisoners) and *King Priam* in which Mark Tatlow and four singers looked both at the sources of the story and at the musical themes that Tippett uses, such as Achilles' war chant, and the motifs of the three Trojan women; and how when they sing together their vocal lines intertwine and merge.

I knew increasingly that an opera company with its pool of singers, and in our case an orchestra made up of soloists, contained within itself the potential talent to perform not just opera but every kind of music, from the symphony to the oratorio, from the solo recital to chamber music – the concert and recital experience feeding and enriching the operatic side of the work and vice versa. The results for the quality of opera, not to mention the widening of its audience were also considerable. Although hindered by shortage of money we had made a significant start with this idea by 1989 with the intention that it should be developed even further in future seasons.

Our longest running series of concerts, begun in 1971, were the Summer Concerts provided for Friends between opera seasons. They were put on in country houses, castles and gardens in Kent and covered a wide range of chamber music, poetry readings and recitals, often with music that fitted the period of the house. I chose the programmes; and the houses, organisation and team of food-makers were provided by two Trust Members, Jane Ross and Elizabeth Ray. The concerts were enormously popular and invariably sold out.

In the eighties I tried to add concerts to the nights of opera in towns or cities that we visited, making of our stay a small festival. To take two examples: when Kent Opera put on a long weekend at the

South Bank in 1987 with Judith Weir's *A Night at the Chinese Opera* and Mozart's *Il Re Pastore*, other events there included *Opera One*, an original entertainment about the beginnings of opera; programmes on 18th century opera and pastorale; readings of pastoral poetry and a chamber concert. At Eastbourne in 1989 when the three operas in the evenings were Monteverdi's *Ulysses*, Beethoven's *Fidelio* and Britten's *Peter Grimes*, the days complemented the evenings with talks, readings and concerts such as *Monteverdi's Madrigals*, directed by Timothy Dean, who was also the pianist in *Winter Words*, settings of Hardy poems by Benjamin Britten, sung by Neil Jenkins. As there was, unusually, no Mozart opera in the repertoire we gave a lunchtime concert of two Mozart quintets, led by the orchestra's leader, Susie Mészáros. There was a programme from the 'Education' series *Fidelio: Prisoners of Conscience*, and Roger Butlin presented an hour on *Ulysses* called *Myth, Music and Design* using a model of his set, two tenors and a theorbo player.

It would have been pleasing for an orchestra as good as Kent's to have been able to rise regularly from pit to stage. The problem was, as always, financial; but in the eighties we did manage a few orchestral concerts. The first was in Dartford and included Mozart's Sinfonia Concertante for violin, viola and orchestra with John Holloway and Nicholas Logie. Then, at the Canterbury Festival, which Robin Jessel and I founded in 1984 and which Kent Opera ran for the first two years, we performed in the first year, British Year, a concert that featured Tippett's *Ritual Dances* (at which the composer was present) and Britten's *Les Illuminations* with Jill Gomez as soloist. The following year, Italian Year, the main item of the Kent Opera concert was Berlioz's *Harold in Italy* with Peter Schidlof as guest violist. And in 1987 we did programmes of Mozart and Beethoven symphonies at the Congress Theatre, Eastbourne, and The Corn Exchange, Cambridge.

One thing I had long wanted to do and (with funds from the Gulbenkian and Clore foundations) was finally able to set up in August 1989 was an in-house training course for singers. Most opera singers enter the profession because they discover they have a good

91

voice. This gift is often linked with some musical ability, more rarely with dramatic ability. In common with other companies – not only in Britain – we found that few singers, however long their studies, entered the profession with more than a rudimentary awareness of the demands of opera performance. The three week intensive training course which I ran with the director Mike Alfreds was intended to be the first of regular annual training sessions. It was limited to fifteen young singers, chosen by audition, and it concentrated on movement and on thinking and imagining truthfully.

And how did we pay for it all? Well, when we opened in 1969, we had a house, bought at auction for a ridiculously low price with a legacy from my wife's grandmother. We also had three newish children: Benjamin, aged four, Rebecca aged two and Lucinda, a few months. With the house came a garden and an oast house (a home for my mother) which after her death we let to Kent Opera as its offices for a peppercorn rent. I continued with my singing and teaching career and my wife, in addition to looking after the children, did some translation of articles and coaching of students for exams. So we could live. The only problem was to find the time and money to raise and establish an opera company. We wrote to all our friends and acquaintances in Kent and many in London telling them that they could become life-members of the as yet unknown and indeed non-existent opera company for the sum of 30 shillings (£1.50) and asking for the names of others who might be interested. Five hundred and fifty people took advantage of this lavish offer – many indeed added donations. And the Arts Council, which in those days had musicians in its Music Department and the flautist John Cruft in charge, added twelve hundred pounds for the first group of performances. There was of course no money for administration – a secretary was employed for odd days and Johanna looked after the press and publicity and I did the sums.

We formed a Trust (as legally required) and invited a number of (mainly) admirable people to sit on it

The usefulness and duties of a Trust are quite difficult to define.
For charities they are of course demanded by law: and it is reasonable
there should be some body to make sure that the executives – i.e. the
professionals who put on the operas and determine the programme –
do not put their hands into the till or commit any other
misdemeanour or act of madness. And Trust Members should also be
enthusiastic, raise money for the company and extend public
awareness of its work. I found that there are people who actually *like*
meetings and that in some cases are simply pleased to have their Trust
Membership noted on their C.V. But an anecdote from the early days
of Kent Opera demonstrates the dangers which a Trust can provide.

We started with the first performances of *Poppea* and followed
these with our production of *Atalanta* at Hintlesham early in 1970.
We had planned and announced three performances of *Figaro* at our
'home base' in Canterbury for the early summer of the same year.
These were immediately sold out. The Arts Council, to whom we
had applied, postponed their decision until after the bookings were
completed and then offered us a grant of half of what we needed.
It was too late to cancel but Kent Opera would be left with what was
for us a rather large deficit. The Trust met to discuss the situation: they
were suitably gloomy but without any practical suggestions. Johanna
and I therefore took out a mortgage on our house to cover the
deficit. The performances of *Figaro* went ahead and were very
successful. The Trust appeared at the following meeting two to three
months later and asked, 'What happened?' I told them and they said,
'Oh, but you shouldn't have!' To which my only possible reply was,
'What the hell then should I have done?' Whereupon the Trust said I
was to enter into no plans for future performances until the mortgage
had been paid off and further funds accumulated. Now this was where
the Trust was both sensible and utterly ignorant: I knew that unless we
went on and planned future performances there was no hope of
getting further funds from the Arts Council or from private sources.
And the whole enterprise would die. This is an example of the

uselessness of well-meaning people, totally ignorant of how the performing arts work. I went ahead with my planning of the next season with *Dido and Aeneas* and our new commission of Alan Ridout's *The Pardoner's Tale* while continuing my search for funding. At the next meeting there were some angry noises and some resignations. Fortunately the subsidies were increased and Kent Opera went on. And those who had forsaken us became our generous friends again. But later on the personnel of the Trust increased and deteriorated and when the big crisis came in the 1980s, when the financial problems of almost every arts establishment became grave, the Trust failed the company altogether.

Meanwhile it was the Arts Council who now encouraged us. It sent regular representatives to the Trust meetings and the performances and after we had been struggling for five to six years, one of these representatives, Donald Ross, suggested to us that we should become Revenue Clients: that is to say that we should make annual applications for the company (and not, as previously, have to apply afresh for each individual production) so that we could make our plans with more accuracy and more confidence (and pay our talented administrative staff better). And we did so. This also meant that we could more successfully raise money from other sources – sponsors, charities, councils and the like. We had an excellent sponsorship record and many of the sponsors, notably Sainsbury's, acted more like acceptable patrons than like unacceptable commercial exploiters. But business sponsors, sometimes a blessing, are not to be depended on – what do you do when the managing director changes and the new one is more interested in ballet than in opera? – What do you do when a bank invited to sponsor *Peter Grimes* says 'No, because it is modern and sad.' Kent Opera's Friends were generous (and in times of crisis magnificent). But of course, in common with the other major opera companies, we depended most heavily on the Arts Council for funding.

I had always said that unless I could interfere in every department

94

and unless I could know everyone in the company, then the company was too big. Obviously one has colleagues to fill the gaps where one is less strong but one shouldn't have large institutions and then say 'How am I going to pour enough stuff into this to fill it?' With the gradual but great increase in work came an increase in staff. But (I was very strict about this) the increase had to be proved to be necessary and our oast house office never contained more than a dozen. One of these was the invaluable Robin Jessel, who had been very doubtful about the enterprise at its beginning; then joined the Trust; and later became an employee, viz our Head of Finance. Here he did a dazzling job not only in managing but in raising funds for the company until 1986, when he retired, and we were fortunate to find a replacement in Michael Flood. Another, earlier member of staff, Graham Allum, was an actor and tenor of much experience: (he was in fact in the original *Poppea* where he met his future wife, Sarah Walker). He decided to change over to administration at a time highly convenient for Kent Opera. He became the General Manager, in which post he was invaluable, bringing with him his inside knowledge and experience of how a theatre company works. He was also unswervingly loyal and supportive.

Because of the compactness of the administration and the fact that all outgoing letters from every department were regularly circulated, everyone was fully aware of and involved in everything that was happening in the company and were free, if they wished, to make comments or ask questions. This made for a democratic office.

In these last two essays I have tried to set out as clearly as possible all the components and priorities of a large musical organisation. The guiding idea of this organisation was to make opera and other forms of music available over a wide geographical area and to ensure the highest quality.

As Jonathan Miller once wrote: 'It was assumed without question that the company was required not only to meet certain standards but actually to set them and in some sense to redefine what opera might be.'

Art made tongue-tied by Authority

But everything we did from 1985 onward both on stage and off was done in the shadow of a threat which culminated in Kent Opera's murder in 1989.

The Arts Council, based on the previous CEMA (Council for the Encouragement of Music and the Arts) – was founded on the creative energy and imagination of J M Keynes and formed by the Attlee government. In a broadcast in July 1945, which launched the Arts Council, Keynes said, 'There could be no better memorial of a war to save the freedom of the spirit of the individual. We look forward to the time when the theatre and the concert-hall and the gallery will be a living element in everyone's upbringing, and regular attendance at the theatre and at concerts a part of organised education.' But despite Keynes, the Arts Council at first proceeded to confine its support mainly to the big London 'flagships' and the leading provincial theatres and orchestras. It felt the need to concentrate its resources, under the illusion that quality would be diluted if spread. The Council did not even fight the Treasury for increased subsidy. All this changed briefly after 1964 when Wilson's Government came in and Jenny Lee became

King Priam Tippett (1984) with Rodney MacCann as King Priam

the first Minister of the Arts with Arnold Goodman as Chairman of the Arts Council. She believed excellence should be universally available and, needing more money to provide this, succeeded in trebling the Arts Council grant from the Treasury in six years. She felt and wrote in her White Paper of 1965, that the job of the state and her own job was to support and then to stand aside; to respond but not to impose and always offer the best to the most.

After she lost her seat in parliament in 1971 there was never another Minister of the Arts like her. For most of her successors it was a job that had to be endured while they waited for a 'better' ministry so they were not too interested in fighting hard for more money for the Arts. (In fact an adequate provision of money should not be a problem: such a small amount in national terms is required, though it needs to be administered with knowledge and imagination.) *The Arts are the most long-lasting and prominent hall-marks of the quality of a civilisation.*

98   1989 was the year in which I had planned to retire. I had appointed Ivan Fischer Music Director in 1982 after he conducted *Agrippina* for us in the same year. He continued to conduct operas of different periods and styles with equal skill and commitment. He was the obvious choice as my successor, though with his world-wide engagements and his own Budapest Festival Orchestra, his answer was in doubt for some time. It was a great relief and satisfaction to me when, feeling that he could combine his international commitments with this position, he finally agreed to take over from me as Artistic Director from 1st October 1989. The Arts Council approved the appointment. And I thought Kent Opera's future was secure.

However, after the advent in 1979 of what *Opera* magazine called 'the most philistine of governments' the Arts Council was increasingly underfunded. As a result talented people of artistic integrity and judgement no longer wanted to work in an institution where making cuts was becoming more common than maintaining grants. The standard of staff deteriorated – no more Crufts, Deanes, Shaws or Fields – and there was an absence of musicians in the Music Department. The

Council's attempts to allocate grants and balance the budget became panic-stricken until it was decided that the only way to cope with the opera budget was to cut a company. And the companies would not unite but each went into its own corner and started fighting its own battle. From 1985 on various 'ideas' were produced – Scottish Opera and Opera North should amalgamate: the cries of indignation from both companies scotched that one. There were two attempts to eliminate Glyndebourne Touring Opera, but influential supporters of the parent company protested vociferously and lo! George Christie became Chairman of the Arts Council Music Panel. Privatisation of Covent Garden was toyed with. Opera 80 (which mounted cut-down opera versions) was threatened, reprieved and eventually renamed English Touring Opera. Then the spotlight was turned on us.

Now Kent was different. We didn't fit. We were also successful and every British performance needed less government subsidy than that demanded by any other opera company. To be different, successful and economical at a time when all the arts are under severe pressure does not always win one friends and perhaps encourages the natural Thatcherite urge to kick in the groin anyone who lacked the political/financial muscle to retaliate. As Graeme Kay wrote in *Classical Music* in January 1990 'It has been common knowledge in the music profession for years that the Council found Kent Opera – its artistic independence fiercely guarded by its now-retired founder Norman Platt – to be an anomaly in the structure of regional opera of which it would rather be rid.' Nor did we downgrade our repertory in accordance with the prevailing fashion in the 1980s (eg. Opera North's *Showboat*) believing, like Lilian Baylis, that if people are given the best they will like it. This was the opposite of the Secretary General of the Arts Council, Luke Rittner's gospel which proclaimed that the most important thing was to get 'bums on seats' by giving the people what they want. How can 'the people' know what they want if they have not been given the opportunity to hear and see the best? As Yeats said to encourage a hesitant sponsor:

'Look up in the sun's eye and give
What the exultant heart calls good
That some new day may breed the best
Because you gave, not what they would
But the right twigs for an eagle's nest.'

This is perhaps the place to mention a theory about 'scale'.
The Arts Council had done a useful survey of theatres in the regions,
dividing them into large-scale, medium-scale and small-scale.
Categorisation of buildings had been transferred effortlessly and
meaninglessly to opera companies and their capabilities. This, of
course, is a ludicrous concept – every opera is as big as the composer
intended and should never be inflated or reduced, as is known to any
intelligent musical person. Nevertheless Kent Opera had to struggle
against the label of 'medium-scale' which an ignorant Arts Council
tried to pin on it. It was angered (we later discovered) by our
mounting *Peter Grimes* which it considered 'large-scale' (and appalled
by a report that I wished to produce *Tristan and Isolde*).

I suppose the final crisis really began on 2nd December 1986
when I was directing *The Seraglio* in Metz. An urgent meeting of
representatives of all seven opera companies (Covent Garden, English
National Opera, Welsh National, Scottish Opera, Glyndebourne
Touring Opera, Opera North and Kent Opera) was called at the Arts
Council and I prepared to fly back for the day. Unfortunately there
was freezing fog and no flights at Luxembourg Airport so Robin Jessel
represented Kent Opera. At the meeting none of the companies had
anything practical to say to the Arts Council's announcement that
there was simply not enough money to go round; except for Nicholas
Payne, then of Opera North, now of ENO via Covent Garden, who
suggested cutting the grant to the City of Birmingham Symphony
Orchestra.

One evening early in 1987 I had an unexpected evening visit from
Kent Opera's Chairwoman and another member of our Trust Council,
who told me on the authority of 'an Arts Council officer' (later

identified by them as Jack Phipps) that unless I resigned immediately the Arts Council subsidy to Kent Opera would be cut off. I questioned the legality and morality of such a threat, and asked what sort of company they would be preserving in such circumstances. And the Secretary General of the Arts Council, Luke Rittner, in his reply to my letter raising these points said: 'I cannot imagine that action of the kind you suggest was taken by any member of the Arts Council staff.' He also expressed his warm admiration for the company's work and thought that the Arts Council's future behaviour to Kent Opera 'will convince you that you have been misinformed in this matter'. He did not mention that at that moment the touring committee 'working-party' was within days of giving birth to the report which was going to recommend the extinction of Kent Opera. Perhaps he forgot.

A few weeks later we were informed by the Arts Council that a report had been written recommending the solution to their opera problems i.e. that Kent Opera should have its grant withdrawn from 1st April 1988.

I went to see Luke Rittner to protest at the contradiction of his recent written statement. He made no answer. I pointed out the quality of our performances. 'We are not concerned with quality' he said, speaking on behalf of the Arts Council. 'Oh dear,' he added, 'perhaps I shouldn't have said that!' I tried a different approach and pointed out to him the indisputable fact that Kent Opera was vastly more economical than any other opera company. He replied 'I don't understand figures.' The working party that had recommended the removal of our grant consisted of 13 people, only two of whom had ever managed to attend a single one of our performances and one of the two was the Director of Scottish Opera, Richard Mantle. But the report was written for them by Jack Phipps. He had been in the Arts Council as Head of Touring but had left in 1982 to 'run' and, as he thought, to reorganise the Aldeburgh Festival. He was however sacked from there in 1984 at short notice and by 1986 was back in the Arts Council, where he urged me repeatedly (always in private, usually after

finance meetings, once in a scribbled note) to use his son as a
conductor for Kent Opera.

We fought Phipps' report and won, partly because of the huge
outcry against it; which was helped by the fact that we were on tour
and were able to appeal to our audiences directly (the letters of protest
were so many that the Arts Council had to employ a new secretary to
answer them); partly because the Friends of Kent Opera (led by
Robin Jessel) promptly raised £60,000 for the Company. And partly
also because Jack Phipps' document, on which the attack was based,
contained so many outrageously false statements that it was easy, once
we got hold of a copy (which was *not* easy) to rubbish it. The Arts
Council Chairman, Sir William Rees-Mogg, would not lay claim to a
profound knowledge of opera but he could smell a rat: and in June
1987 the report was quashed and Jack Phipps was forced to apologise
to the Chairman for issuing misleading information.

(From Opera North Nicholas Payne commented: 'The whole
idea was that Norman would want to call it a day and we could have
his money.')

That same month Kent Opera performed one of its most valuable
services to opera in this country – the production of Judith Weir's
A Night at the Chinese Opera which we commissioned with funds
provided by the BBC. It was a work of outstanding musical and
dramatic originality, the many-layered tragi-comic story of a young
man who collaborated with the Mongols in 13th century China.
The press were unable to fault it. The following quotes were typical
of their reactions: 'Judith Weir's new opera is simply brilliant, brilliantly
simple, fresh, colourful and enchanting and quite the wittiest thing to
be done in the musical theatre for years. ... This is the debut of a very
remarkable composer.' (The Times). 'There cannot have been many
better examples of a creative collaboration and Kent Opera could not
have found a more compelling reason for survival.' (The Guardian)
It would have been difficult even for the Arts Council to cut us at
that moment.

Also in 1987 the Arts Council acknowledged that we needed an increase of subsidy of at least £100,000 on top of the annual (but frozen) grant of £750,000 and indeed they offered that sum – but withdrew the offer one week later.

In 1988 we did our two English tours (which included *Count Ory, A Night at the Chinese Opera, Don Giovanni* and *Fidelio*) and then we were the first British company to be invited to Singapore to put on *Don Giovanni* for three nights to full houses of Singaporeans with a refreshing lack of preconceptions about how to react to opera. Their spontaneous enjoyment was wonderful. As Keith Clarke of Classical Music said, 'The atmosphere in the hall was the stuff that opera companies' dreams are made of.' Later that year we visited Valencia in Spain with *Don Giovanni* and *Fidelio*.

It was a good year and recognised as such. 'It was the first regional company in England. It pioneered the education 'Outreach'. It is zealous in fund-raising. All in all the Arts Council has reason to be pleased with Kent Opera' wrote the Sunday Times. 'Artistically Kent Opera's overall track record during its existence has been outstanding' wrote The Telegraph.

But at the Arts Council there were still those who, for their own reasons, wanted to get rid of Kent Opera: these included Jack Phipps, Graham Marchant (Director: Arts Co-ordination) and Anthony Everitt (Deputy Secretary General), who later said on radio that he could judge performances

Fidelio Beethoven (1982) The prisoners' chorus

by reading about them in the newspapers. Sir William Rees-Mogg retired as Chairman and was followed by Peter Palumbo who, in 1989, came to the first night of *Peter Grimes* in Canterbury and immediately wrote me the following hand-written thank you letter: 'I am writing to say how much I enjoyed the first night of *Peter Grimes* at The Marlowe yesterday evening; and to thank you for such kind and generous hospitality, and for a wonderfully warm welcome. It was altogether a memorable experience made even more so by meeting you for the first time; and I am both full of admiration, and deeply in your debt.' That was before he went back to the Arts Council office and found that he was out of step with the party line.

Our reprieve in 1987 had not been without conditions. Our grant from the Arts Council had been deliberately frozen for the previous three years and in 1983, after the Priestley report, the much larger accumulated deficits of the other companies had been paid off: but not Kent's. Now we were required to raise a further £200,000 ourselves. We had an Achilles heel in that we had less financial support from local authorities than any other company (except perhaps Scottish Opera): Dartford was generous, Canterbury gave nothing and Kent County Council did not support us strongly enough. Luke Rittner began a correspondence with Tony Hart, Chairman of Kent County Council, and Mr Hart agreed that their support was indeed inadequate; he promised to try to get it raised from £22,500 per annum to £60,000 rising to £200,000 per year – if the Arts Council would guarantee to continue its support for Kent Opera. Unfortunately by December 1989 the KCC grant had risen to only £45,000. (When the axe fell KCC desperately worked out how to raise the £200,000 but was told by the Arts Council it was too late.)

I retired in September 1989. The office moved from our oast house to a 16th century building in Dartford provided by Dartford Council. Ivan Fischer made a three year plan which included foreign (particularly French) tours, a new *Cosi fan Tutte* to be directed by Mike Alfreds, and two new opera premieres – one by Peter Maxwell Davies

(Previous page) **A Night at the Chinese Opera** Weir (1987) with, top, Michael Chance, bottom from left to right, Alan Oke, Jonathan Best, Frances Lynch, David Johnston, Diccon Cooper, Tomos Ellis and Enid Hartle

and the other *Baa Baa Black Sheep* by Michael Berkeley – but first
of all I had arranged for three performances in February 1990 of
our production of Michael Tippett's *King Priam* directed by Nicholas
Hytner and to be conducted by Ivan himself at Covent Garden as an
85th birthday tribute to Kent Opera's President and England's most
famous living composer. (This, of course, made nonsense of the Arts
Council's 'middle scale' theory.)

I had warned Ivan not to put too much faith in the words of the
Arts Council but he was used to dealing with the corruption of a
communist regime; he thought the British system was clean and fairly
honourable. The company consulted the Arts Council at every stage
of the plan and Jack Phipps (again) advised Fischer to make it more
ambitious and to visit more theatres on the tour, increasing the annual
number of planned performances in England from 43 to 61. (This
would require a larger grant from the Arts Council but a smaller
subsidy per performance.) Fischer altered the estimates accordingly.

Then in December 1989, a week after the Arts Council received
an extra £20 million to spend on the Arts, the axe fell. It was
announced that Kent Opera's three year plan was too ambitious,
expensive and ill thought out; that Kent Opera's artistic standards
of late had fallen (this accusation was later retracted) and that Kent
Opera's future grant would be withdrawn, thus ensuring that not
a single work by the new (Arts Council approved) Artistic Director
could be mounted.

This announcement had been achieved by presenting the
music panel, an advisory and unpaid group of people with musical
interests, with an item on Kent Opera at its meeting. This item was
not listed, there were no papers available for reference, and there was
pressure from officers of the Arts Council for a decision in favour of
a cut. The panel (chaired by George Christie of Glyndebourne)
bowed to the pressure and advised the cutting of Kent Opera's grant.
Robert Ponsonby, former BBC controller of music (who had been
unable to attend the panel meeting) resigned, saying 'I am personally

disillusioned about the Arts Council's advisory system. On this particular occasion the music panel was not briefed at all about a major item, it was not on the agenda. ... I don't really want any more voluntarily to give time and effort to the Arts Council when one is not properly briefed, one's advice is often rejected or ignored and one is misrepresented.' Former Arts Council music officer Stephen Firth wrote to the Guardian: 'As I attended meetings over the years I frequently observed respected and knowledgeable representatives of the music profession being treated in what I can only describe as an off-hand manner and often lacking enough information to enable them to give informed, objective advice. This is in conformity with a trend in the arts bureaucracy towards what is quaintly known as 'generalism'; translated this means that credence is given to those with minimal knowledge of the arts, but some skill in, for example, marketing, rather than those who have spent a lifetime working in the field.'

I have never known such a firm negative given to any Arts Council proposal as that given by a galaxy of distinguished composers, conductors, directors, singers and audiences. Michael Tippett wrote an article for *The Guardian* in which he described the Arts Council's action as 'inept, devious and high-handed' and said that 'the barest survey of Kent Opera's achievements and future potential must indeed inspire everyone to defend them and put pressure on the Arts Council to reverse the recent decision.' The Duke of Kent went to 105 Piccadilly to see the Arts Council Chairman Peter Palumbo and plead for the Company of which he was patron.

All were ignored. The cut was confirmed.

'All have gone', wrote Rodney Milnes in *Opera*, of Kent's future plans, 'and with them at a single stroke ... artistic standards unsurpassed in this country.'

The behaviour of Kent's operatic colleagues in the touring field was once more distressing, if not entirely amazing. Richard Mantle of Scottish Opera had already helped increase our deficit by reneging on an agreed joint production of *Count Ory*, leaving us with the full cost. ('There's nothing in writing ', he said.) There was unsupportive silence from others. 'I suppose I should protest?' said Brian MacMaster, then of Welsh National Opera, now of the Edinburgh Festival, with a smile. 'I judged silence to be better than piss and wind' wrote Nicholas Payne, then still at Opera North, in a self-justifying letter to *Opera* magazine. Kent Opera's grant when divided between the other six companies (and Opera 80) did not go far, but George Christie immediately appropriated our orchestra for Glyndebourne Touring Opera.

So what had all this dishonesty in the Arts Council, aided and abetted by other Arts Organisations, achieved? It had lost Britain a major opera company and one of today's great conductors. Ivan left Britain at once and returns only occasionally with his Budapest Festival Orchestra or to conduct the Orchestra of the Age of Enlightenment or to appear at the Proms.

I have written this to demonstrate that the destruction of Kent Opera, a company which made a unique and irreplaceable contribution to the Arts, was a senseless act which involved highly dishonest behaviour in a public body.

The moral of this true story is that people of knowledge, talent and integrity can spend twenty years building and developing a large, successful musical organisation. And fools and liars can destroy it in days.

The Arts are essential to a civilised country; they should be subsidised by the government generously but not wastefully; an Arts Council should be staffed and guided by honest people with the appropriate knowledge and experience of the different arts; and the arts companies themselves should be run by people with adequate professional experience and commitment and not by so-called managers and administrators. Twelve years on this has not happened.

The Arts are a necessity not a luxury.

109

Coda

But this was not quite the end. In 1990 Mark Deller of the
Canterbury Festival invited us to put on a Memorial Concert for Kent
Opera – we accepted but only if it was a <u>Celebration</u> Concert. Ivan
and the orchestra returned and many of our singers and our chorus
took part in appropriate excerpts from past productions, including
the finale of *Fidelio*. Two new works were written for the occasion:
Ridout's *Flourish: Audite Haec Omnes* and Weir's *Ox Mountain was
covered by Trees*, while Tippett's song cycle *The Heart's Assurance* in
a new orchestration by Meirion Bowen was also performed. The
concert was sold out and at the end the company was given a standing
ovation. All the performers waived their fees, knowing that my
pension had gone with the company, so that the box office receipts of
£9,000 came to me. With my usual disregard for my family but with
Johanna's agreement and help I used the money to restart Kent Opera,
first with a series of concerts of linked music and poetry called the
Janus Series, with three children's/community operas, and then, in
1994, with a tour of Britten's *The Prodigal Son*, directed by Tim Carroll
under the musical direction of Timothy Dean, which started at the
Bath Festival, toured churches and cathedrals and ended with a
performance at St John's Smith Square recorded by the BBC. This was
as perfect as anything done in earlier days and was followed the next
year, the tricentenary of Purcell's death, by a tour of *The Masque in
Dioclesian* and then a new production of Monteverdi's *Orfeo* in 1997/8
ending at the Bath Festival.

I handed over again in 1996 to Roger Butlin, Tim Carroll and
John Toll with a Trust headed by John Macdonald QC. Now it is
up to them.

The Prodigal Son Britten (1994) with Alan Watt as the Father and James Oxley as
the Younger Son

Epilogue

The second half of the 20th century began musically in 1945 with the creative triumph of *Peter Grimes* together with the hopes that this aroused (many of which were fulfilled in the following years); the 1940s also witnessed the concrete achievements of the early Third Programme and the early Arts Council leading to the bright-eyed optimism of the Festival of Britain. And this was the first time ever in Britain that the country had a government which believed that the Arts mattered and acted upon that belief – and that belief and that action came from a government faced with the enormous pressures of post-war chaos and the revolutionary establishment of a National Health Service.

Labour under Wilson continued with this belief. And then in 1979 came Margaret Thatcher and the downgrading of everything that did not make money. This was not a new attitude: 'The fact is England is strictly and decidedly commercial and the highest gifts of genius are considered more in the light of curses than blessings if a man puts forth his powers on any principle incompatible with the commercial basis of sale and returns' – a complaint made by the painter Benjamin Haydon in 1828.

When Labour returned in 1997, hope returned. But the bitterness

Orfeo Monteverdi (1976) with Peter Knapp as Orfeo and Rosalind Plowright as the Messenger

is, that although this government purports to descend from the same source as that of the 1945 government and has the inestimable advantage of following and contrasting with the squalidness of its immediate predecessors, it too avoids making any real quality or value judgements. In fact it shows its unawareness by the quite ludicrous inclusive title given to the Arts Minister (Minister of Arts, Media and Sport). This blurring of three unconnected fields is a tribute to the fading fad of relativism (ie. the view that everything is equally good, equally trivial, equally bad, equally valuable). Instead of putting much more money into music and drama teaching; arts education, exhibitions and performances; making available to the young and the unaware the best in all the arts (as in 1951), the policy seems to be inanely to downgrade works of quality. Judgements in the arts have to be made on the grounds of quality and those judging need to have the expertise and passion of artistic professionals. Which was not the case in 1989 nor is it now with either of the two main parties or the present shambles still known as the Arts Council.

I have said that the only thing that counts in music is quality – quality of the material and quality of the performance. This is of course to beg quite a number of questions since quality is not a thing which can be proved.

It can however be recognised.

And this recognition contains elements of wonder, delight, enlightenment and perhaps awe. It is a revelation. It comes from outside, 'over there'.

As Iris Murdoch said, 'The art object conveys, in the most accessible and for many the only available form, the idea of a transcendent perfection. Great art inspires because it is separate, it is for nothing, it is for itself. It is an image of virtue. Its condensed, clarified presentation enables us to look without sin upon a sinful world.'

Or, in Oscar Wilde's words 'all art is quite useless' – except of course insofar as it provides a standard of beauty and value and human worth which can be found nowhere else.

114

Kent Opera Performances 1969–1989

	Production	Composer	Librettist	Conductor
116	The Coronation of Poppea	Monteverdi	Francesco Busenello H. Proctor-Gregg (tr)	Roger Norrington
	Atalanta	Handel	Unknown N. Platt & L. Sarti (tr)*	Roger Norrington
	The Marriage of Figaro	Mozart	Lorenzo Da Ponte E.J. Dent (tr)	Roger Norrington
	Dido and Aeneas	Purcell	Nahum Tate	Roger Norrington
	The Pardoner's Tale (commissioned by K.O.)	Ridout	Norman Platt	Roger Norrington
	Venus and Adonis	Blow	unknown	Meredith Davies
	Don Giovanni	Mozart	Lorenzo Da Ponte N. Platt & L.Sarti (tr)*	Roger Norrington
	HMS Pinafore	Sullivan	W.S. Gilbert	Roger Norrington Nicholas Kraemer Jonathan Hinden
	The Coronation of Poppea	Monteverdi	Francesco Busenello N. Platt (tr)*	Roger Norrington
	The Patience of Socrates (1st professional UK performance)	Telemann	J. U. Von Konig N. Platt & J. Froom(tr)*	Roger Norrington
	Cosi Fan Tutte	Mozart	Lorenzo Da Ponte R. & T. Martin (tr)	Roger Norrington Jonathan Hinden
	Ruddigore	Sullivan	W.S. Gilbert	Roger Norrington

* denotes commissioned translation

Producer	Designer	Lighting	Year	
Norman Platt	Nadine Baylis	Neil Foster	1969	117
Norman Platt	Jean Jones	Peter Harwood	1970	
Norman Platt	Jane Kingshill	Peter Harwood	1970	
Norman Platt	Peter Harwood	Peter Harwood	1971	
Norman Platt	Peter Harwood	Peter Harwood	1971	
Norman Platt	Jean Jones	Peter Harwood	1972	
Norman Platt	Michael Day & Frances Nerini	Peter Harwood	1972	
Adrian Slack	Frances Nerini	Peter Harwood	1973	
Norman Platt	Jean Jones	Peter Harwood	1974	
Norman Platt	Frances Nerini	Peter Harwood	1974	
Jonathan Miller	Bernard Culshaw	Nick Chelton	1974	
Adrian Slack	David Fielding	Andrew Bridge	1975	

Production	Composer	Librettist	Conductor
Rigoletto	Verdi	Francesco Maria Piave	Roger Norrington
		J. Machlis (tr)	Jonathan Hinden
The Magic Flute	Mozart	Emanuel Schikaneder	Roger Norrington
		M. Irwin (tr)*	
Venus and Adonis	Blow	unknown	Roger Norrington
The Pardoner's Tale	Ridout	Norman Platt	Roger Norrington
Orfeo	Monteverdi	Alessandro Striggio	Roger Norrington
		A.Ridler (tr)*	
Eugene Onegin	Tchaikovsky	Tchiaikovsky &	Roger Norrington
		Konstantin Shilovsky	Jonathan Hinden
		M.Irwin (tr)*	
Iphigenia in Tauris	Gluck	Nicolas Francois	Roger Norrington
		Guillard	
		M.Irwin (tr)*	
The Seraglio	Mozart	Christoph Friedrich	Roger Norrington
		Bietzner	Jonathan Hinden
		M. Irwin (tr)*	
The Return of Ulysses	Monteverdi	Giaconio Badoaro	Roger Norrington
		A.Ridler (tr)*	
Idomeneo	Mozart	Abbé Varesco	Roger Norrington
		M. Irwin (tr)*	
La Traviata	Verdi	Francesco Maria Piave	Roger Norrington
		M.Irwin (tr)*	
The Turn of the Screw	Britten	Myfanwy Piper	Roger Norrington
Venus & Adonis	Blow	Unknown	Roger Norrington
Il Ballo delle Ingrate	Monteverdi	Rinuccini	Roger Norrington
		A. Ridler (tr)*	
The Magic Flute	Mozart	Schikaneder	Roger Norrington
		M. Irwin (tr)*	
Falstaff	Verdi	Boito	Roger Norrington
		M.Irwin (tr)*	
La Traviata	Verdi	Piave	Roger Norrington
		M. Irwin (tr)*	
Turn of the Screw	Britten	Myfanwy Piper	Roger Norrington
Cosi Fan Tutte	Mozart	Lorenzo Da Ponte	Timothy Dean
		R & T Martin (tr)	
Venus & Adonis	Blow	Unknown	Roger Norrington
Il Ballo delle Ingrate	Monteverdi	Rinuccini	Roger Norrington
		A. Ridler (tr)*	
Falstaff	Verdi	Boito	Roger Norrington

Producer	Designer	Lighting	Year
Jonathan Miller	Bernard Culshaw	Nick Chelton	1975
Norman Platt	Martyn Bainbridge	Nick Chelton	1976
Norman Platt	Jean Jones	Nick Chelton	1976
Norman Platt	Peter Harwood	Peter Harwood	1976
Jonathan Miller	Bernard Culshaw	Nick Chelton	1976
Jonathan Miller	Bernard Culshaw	Nick Chelton	1977
Norman Platt	Roger Butlin	Nick Chelton	1977
Elijah Moshinsky	Deirdre Clancy	Nick Chelton	1978
Norman Platt	Roger Butlin	Nick Chelton	1978
Norman Platt	Roger Butlin	Nick Chelton	1979
Jonathan Miller	Bernard Culshaw	Nick Chelton	1979
Nicholas Hytner	Douglas Heap	Mark Henderson	1979
Norman Platt & Christopher Bruce	Jean Jones	Nick Chelton	1980
Christopher Bruce	Nadine Baylis	Nick Chelton	1980
Norman Platt	Martyn Bainbridge	Nick Chelton	1980
Jonathan Miller	Bernard Culshaw	Nick Chelton	1980
Jonathan Miller	Bernard Culshaw	Nick Chelton	1980
Nicholas Hytner	Douglas Heap	Mark Henderson	1980
Jonathan Miller	Bernard Culshaw	Nick Chelton	1981
Norman Platt	Jean Jones	Nick Chelton	1981
Christopher Bruce	Nadine Baylis	Nick Chelton	1981
Jonathan Miller	Bernard Culshaw	Nick Chelton	1981

Production	Composer	Librettist	Conductor
Il Combattimento di Tancredi e Clorinda	Monteverdi	Monteverdi	Roger Norrington
Lettera Amorosa	Monteverdi	Monteverdi	Roger Norrington
The Marriage of Figaro	Mozart	Da Ponte M. Irwin (tr)*	Roger Norrington
Eugene Onegin	Tchaikovsky	Tchaikovsky/Schilovsky M. Irwin (tr)*	Roger Norrington
Agrippina	Handel	Grimani Anne Ridler (tr)	Ivan Fischer
Eugene Onegin	Tchaikovsky	Tchaikovsky/Schilovsky M.Irwin (tr)*	Roger Norrington
The Marriage of Figaro	Mozart	Da Ponte M. Irwin (tr)*	Roger Norrington
The Beggar's Opera	arr. Britten	Gay	Peter Robinson
Fidelio	Beethoven	Sonnleithner/Treitschke N. Platt (tr)*	Roger Norrington
The Beggar's Opera	arr. Britten	Gay	Peter Robinson
Fidelio	Beethoven	Soinnleithner N.Platt (tr)*	Roger Norringlon
Don Giovanni	Mozart	Da Ponte N. Platt/L. Sarti (tr)*	Peter Robinson
Robinson Crusoe	Offenbach	Cormon & Cremieux Don White (tr)	Roger Norrington
Falstaff	Verdi	Boito M. Irwin(tr)*	Roger Norrington
The Seraglio	Mozart	C. F. Bretzner M. Irwin (tr)*	Ivan Fischer
Robinson Crusoe	Offenbach	Cormon & Cremieux Don White (tr)	Roger Norrington
Falstaff	Verdi	Boito M. Irwin (tr)*	Roger Norrington
King Priam	Tippett	Tippett	Roger Norrington
The Marriage of Figaro	Mozart	Da Ponte M. Irwin(tr)*	Ivan Fischer
The Barber of Seville	Rossini	Sterbini M. Irwin (tr)*	Arnold Östmann
King Priam	Tippett	Tippett	Roger Norrington
The Marriage of Figaro	Mozart	Da Ponte M. Irwin (tr)*	Graeme Jenkins
Agrippina	Handel	Grimani A.Ridler (tr)*	Ivan Fischer

Producer	Designer	Lighting	Year
Christopher Bruce	Pamela Marre	Nick Chelton	1981
Norman Platt	Pamela Marre	Nick Chelton	1981
Nicholas Hytner	David Fielding	Nick Chelton	1981
Jonathan Miller	Bernard Culshaw	Nick Chelton	1981
Norman Platt & Christopher Bruce	Roger Butlin	Nick Chelton	1982
Jonathan Miller	Bernard Culshaw	Nick Chelton	1982
Nicholas Hytner	David Fielding	Nick Chelton	1982
Nicholas Hytner	Di Seymour	Nick Chelton	1982
Jonathan Miller	Bernard Culshaw	Nick Chelton	1982
Nicholas Hytner	Di Seymour	Nick Chelton	1983
Jonathan Miller	Bernard Culshaw	Nick Chelton	1983
Adrian Noble	Bob Crowley	Mark Henderson	1983
Adrian Slack	Dermot Hayes	Mark Pritchard	1983
Jonathan Miller	Bernard Culshaw	Nick Chelton	1983
Norman Platt	Roger Butlin	Nick Chelton	1984
Adrian Slack	Dermot Hayes	Mark Pritchard	1984
Jonathan Miller	Bernard Culshaw	Nick Chelton	1984
Nicholas Hytner	David Fielding	Paul Pyant	1984
Nicholas Hytner	David Fielding	Nick Chelton	1984
Jonathan Hales	Roger Butlin	Nick Chelton	1985
Nicholas Hytner	David Fielding	Paul Pyant	1985
Nicholas Hytner	David Fielding	Nick Chelton	1985
Norman Platt	Roger Butlin	Nick Chelton	1985

Production	Composer	Librettist	Conductor
La Traviata	Verdi	Piave M. Irwin (tr)*	Ivan Fischer
The Coronation of Poppea	Monteverdi	Busenello N. Platt (tr)*	Ivan Fischer
La Traviata	Verdi	Piave M. Irwin (tr)*	Ivan Fischer
The Marriage of Figaro	Mozart	Da Ponte M. Irwin (tr)*	Graeme Jenkins
Dido & Aeneas	Purcell	NahumTate	Mark Tatlow
Pygmalion	Rameau	de Sorot A. Ridler (tr)*	Mark Tatlow
Carmen	Bizet	Meilhac & Halévy M. Irwin (tr)*	Ivan Fischer
Dido & Aeneas	Purcell	Nahum Tate	Andrew Parrott
Pygmalion	Rameau	de Sorot A. Ridler (tr)*	Andrew Parrott
Carmen	Bizet	Meilhac & Halévy M. Irwin (tr)	Ivan Fischer
The Magic Flute	Mozart	Schikaneder M. Irwin (tr)*	Ivan Fischer
A Night at the Chinese Opera (commissioned by K.O.)	Weir	Weir	Andrew Parrott
Il Re Pastore	Mozart	Metastasio A. Ridler (tr)*	Ivan Fischer
Count Ory	Rossini	Scribe & Delestre- Poirson M. Irwin (tr)*	Ivan Fischer/ Timothy Dean
A Night at the Chinese Opera	Weir	Weir	Andrew Parrott
Don Giovanni	Mozart	Da Ponte N. Platt/L. Sarti (tr)*	Ivan Fisher
Fidelio	Beethoven	Sonnleithner/Treitschke N. Platt (tr)*	Ivan Fischer
The Return of Ulysses	Monteverdi	Giacomo Badoaro A. Ridler (tr)*	John Toll
Peter Grimes	Britten	Montague Slater	Ivan Fischer
The Burning Fiery Furnace	Britten	William Plomer	Timothy Dean

During this period there were also regular chamber and orchestral concerts.

Producer	Designer	Lighting	Year
Adrian Slack	Bernard Culshaw	Nick Chelton	1985
Jonathan Hales	Roger Butlin	Gerry Amies	1986
Adrian Slack	Bernard Culshaw	Nick Chelton	1986
Nicholas Hytner	David Fielding	Nick Chelton	1986
Mary Forey	Roger Butlin	Nick Chelton	1986
Mary Forey	Roger Butlin	Nick Chelton	1986
Robin Lefèvre	Grant Hicks	Gerry Jenkinson	1986
Norman Platt	Roger Butlin	Nick Chelton	1987
Mary Forey	Roger Butlin	Nick Chelton	1987
Robin Lefèvre	Grant Hicks	Gerry Jenkinson	1987
Robert Knights	Roger Butlin	Nick Chelton	1987
Richard Jones	Richard Hudson	Nick Chelton	1987
Michael McCarthy	Roger Butlin	Ace McCarron	1987
Richard Jones	Richard Hudson	Nick Chelton	1988
Richard Jones	Richard Hudson	Nick Chelton	1988
Norman Platt	Bob Crowley	Mark Henderson	1988
Ian Watt-Smith	Bernard Culshaw	Nick Chelton	1988
Thomas Hemsley	Roger Butlin	Paul Pyant	1989
Norman Platt	Bernard Culshaw	Nick Chelton	1989
Ian Watt-Smith	Mark Hinton	Ian Watt-Smith	1989

Performances 1994–1998

Production	Composer	Librettist	Conductor
The Prodigal Son	Britten	William Plomer	Timothy Dean
The Masque in Dioclesian	Purcell	Thomas Betterton	Michael Rosewell
Orfeo	Monteverdi	Alessandro Striggio	John Toll

These operas were preceded in 1991 by a series of concerts of words and music
all interlinked and entitled the Janus Series.

Producer	Designer	Lighting	Year	
Tim Carroll	Roger Butlin	Simon Opie	1994	125
Tim Carroll	Roger Butlin	Simon Opie	1995	
Tim Carroll	Roger Butlin	Jonathan Driscoll	1997	

Kent Opera Commissions

Production	Composer	Librettist	Conductor
The Pardoner's Tale	Alan Ridout	Norman Platt	Roger Norrington
Angelo*	Alan Ridout	Johanna & Norman Platt	Roger Norrington
Dr Syn*	Adrian Cruft	Johanna Platt	
The Black Spider*	Judith Weir	Judith Weir	
A Night at the Chinese Opera	Judith Weir	Judith Weir	Andrew Parrott
The Two Lockets*	Christopher Brown	Bob Devereux	Christopher Brown

In addition to the above operas, Michael Irwin was commissioned to write a play on the life of Rossini, for two actors/singers and piano, using the music from the Barber of Seville.

A Gift at Christmas*	Ruth Byrchmore	Johanna Platt	Ruth Byrchmore
Baba Yaga*	Ruth Byrchmore	Johanna Platt	Martin Handley

NB: only professional participants listed

*Children's Opera written to be performed by children and young people with one or two professional singers.

Producer	Designer	Lighting	Year
Norman Platt	Peter Harwood	Peter Harwood	1971
Nadia de Lichtenberg	Francis Pym		1971
Mary Forey	Roger Butlin		1983
Amanda Knott		Dee Ashworth	1985
Richard Jones	Richard Hudson	Nick Chetton	1987
Patrick Young	Clare Young		1988
Mary Forey	Roger Butlin		1992
Amanda Knott	Roger Butlin & Louisa Beer	Simon Opie	1995

Cupid Etching by Jane Lewis
used on the posters for
A Masque in Dioclesian by
Purcell (1985)